COVERT CULTURE SOURCEBOOK

Also by Richard Kadrey

Metrophage

Signal: Communication Tools for the Information Age (co-editor)

Kamikaze L'Amour (forthcoming)

About the author:

Richard Kadrey was born in Brooklyn in 1957, and now lives in San Francisco. He has no qualifications for anything he does.

COVERT CULTURE SOURCEBOOK

by Richard Kadrey

ST. MARTIN'S PRESS   NEW YORK

COVERT CULTURE SOURCEBOOK

Portions of this book have appeared previously in *Science Fiction Eye*, *bOING-bOING* and *Whole Earth Review*.

Design by David Barker.

Library of Congress Cataloging-in-Publication Data

Kadrey, Richard.
    Covert culture sourcebook / Richard Kadrey.
         p.   cm.
    ISBN 0-312-09776-X
    1. Social history—1970- 2. Civilization, Modern—1950-
3. Subculture.   I. Title.
HN17.5.K33   1993
306—dc20   93-2563
                                      CIP

First Edition: September 1993
10 9 8 7 6 5 4 3 2 1

Acknowledgements

My appreciation goes to a number of people for helping me finish something that started as a smart-ass conceit and ended as this book. I'd like to thank David Barker for making the book look so good, Ellen Klages for making the text much less random, editors Gordon Van Gelder and Bill Thomas for their encouragement, wholly undeserved trust and suggestions and my agent, Merrilee Heifetz, for convincing me to do the book in the first place.

I'd like to thank all the writers who contributed, especially Mark Faigenbaum, Mary Maxwell and Paco Xander Nathan, who went above and beyond the call of data-gathering and review-writing. Also Jeanne Carstensen and Kevin Kelly of the *Whole Earth Review*, who hired me to edit the column that got me up close and personal with covert culture. And, finally, members of the WELL online community in the Bay Area for answering questions and providing addresses when I was in a corner.

This book is dedicated to Pat (get used to it), and to Eva, who wanted more and got it.

Contents

The Revolution Will Be Faxed:
An Introduction

Nothing interesting ever happens at the center. Everything interesting is out at the edges. Sparks kick up when two edges meet. Sometimes hot edges fuse, creating something weird and new—the birth of a hopeful monster.

Beats, Hippies, Yippies, Punks—they were the extremists, the monsters, the dangerous edge against which the rest of culture was judged. But time moves on and the range of acceptable culture has expanded to include these earlier aberrants, drawing them toward the center. Punk is now an automobile marketing scheme. William Burroughs is a Gap ad. Jerry Rubin gave up fighting cops to fight cholesterol on his Stair Master. It's not their fault. The media maw gobbles up trends and ideas so fast that what seemed hot at breakfast is just empty jars of Cheez-Whiz by lunch. So where the hell is the edge now?

The answer is simple: *there is no edge*. There never really has been. Or rather, there are a thousand edges, at a thousand different angles to each other. Until recently, though, that wasn't always easy to see. It's communication technology that's letting us get up close and personal with the razor's edge of thought. Copying machines, digital samplers, videocams and computers are the tools of the edge explorers. Anarchists don't throw bombs anymore. They mix them into songs. Or post them on computer bulletin boards.

The new monsters—zine publishers, renegade video artists, underground sysops, fashion mobsters—have always been there, but they couldn't make themselves heard over the noise of network TV, MOR radio and glossy magazines. Now anyone with a computer and a printer can be her or his own magazine, computer bulletin board or recording studio. In fact, that annoying buzz in the background of the mainstream media barrage just might be a pirate radio station whispering between the frequencies, birthing new monsters, spewing memes like thought-viruses into the ether.

That's Covert Culture. Covert Culture is the unexplored terrain that's been right in front of you all along, but was impossible to see.

The **Covert Culture Sourcebook** is a guide to alternative music, books, video, zines and tools for living. It's a starter kit, a sort of treasure map where X doesn't mark the spot, but a thousand Xs mark a thousand spots. Start digging anywhere that looks interesting. Who knows what you might find? Maybe—if you look hard enough—it will be something you didn't expect, but have always been looking for.

If you have suggestions, updates, verbal abuse or items you'd like to see reviewed in future incarnations of the **Covert Culture Sourcebook**, you can send them to:

Richard Kadrey
c/o Covert Culture Sourcebook
2440 16th St.
P.O. Box 229
San Francisco, CA 94103

books

Introduction—Books

Like the music biz, book publishing is being transformed by independent entrepreneurs, cheap production facilities, and microelectronics. Computer-based DTP (desktop publishing) means that anyone with a moderately powerful word-processing program can be a miniature Max Perkins—producing and acquiring original work, then packaging and distributing it through in other small-scale publications—mainly zines. The micro-publisher doesn't even need a publicity budget, because zine ads are often traded, not bought. The effect this has had on big-time publishing is subtle, but viral, and its effects are still spreading.

In a mutate-or-die environment, the smart grow extra legs and learn to foxtrot in a whole new way. Take the book you're holding in your hands (literally, if you want; I get royalties whether you buy it or steal it). The **Covert Culture Sourcebook** is one of a growing number of text-based chimeras—a DTP creation in major publishing house drag. And there are more and more of these cross-bred monsters out there, because not only are major publishers picking up independent DTP works, but writers who ordinarily go to big publishing houses are finding a warm reception for their less commercial work at the small press end of the food chain (check out John Shirley's **New Noir**, page 18).

In this looser publishing environment, a whole range of twisted books and personal obsessions have bubbled to the surface like gas in a tar pit. New titles on topics such as crime, drugs, politics, history, ideas of place, science, sexuality and art—in treatments both millennial and conventional—appear every day. A few notable ones are reviewed in this Books section.

A new type of fiction has also appeared in this information-heavy environment, probably born less from something like DTP and more from the culture that created it. This fiction has been dubbed "slipstream," a term coined by Bruce Sterling and Richard Dorsett. Slipstream refers to a kind of postmodern fiction that defies easy genre classification. It often combines elements of older genres, such as science fiction and mystery, with high literary concerns and style. As a school of fiction, it's a cultural mongrel, splicing fantastic, sometimes deliberately surreal images and ideas with journalistic snapshots of contemporary life, all designed to undercut many of our assumptions about everyday reality. Most of the slipstream titles reviewed here, such as **Easy Travel to Other Planets** and **Waiting for the End of the World** (see reviews on pages 14 and 7, respectively), take nothing for granted—including their own existence as works of fiction. They are sometimes unsettling to read, leaving you with a kind of restless desire to find out *just what the hell is going on here*. It's the slipstream novel's sense of the unreality of life at the end of the twentieth century that's its primary power. After all, in an era when the wrong kind of sex can kill you, and where a sweep of the TV dial can get you live coverage of ethnic cleansing in the Balkans, "The Brady Bunch," the Home Shopping Network and presidential candidates debating the morals of fictional characters, who's to say where reality lies anymore?

Portrait of an Eye

by Kathy Acker
$15; Pantheon Books
1992; 310 pp.

Like the noted eighteenth-century jailbird and author, the Marquis de Sade, Kathy Acker is a relentlessly misunderstood writer. The confusion began early in her career, and you can see why in this trilogy of her early books.

The first book, The Childlike Life of the Black Tarantula by the Black Tarantula, opens with the line, "I become a murderess." First person, present tense, right in your face. The book is one long, twisted experiment with the word "I" as text and identity. Acker went to the library and got the goods on a host of famous female Victorian killers. Like the drag queens she hung with when she wrote the book, she got into violent Victorian drag, rewriting the women's stories as autobiography and placing the stolen material next to parts of real autobiography.

Acker is at heart a conceptualist, not the romantic image of the artist who flies away on wings of inspirations. The other books in Portrait of an Eye were also well-conceived experiments. Both I Dreamt I Was a Nymphomaniac: Imagining and The Adult Life of Toulouse-Lautrec by Henri Toulouse-Lautrec use the basic method of her first book—"I" placed against real and stolen texts—but extend the idea into the areas of memory, pornography and politics.

By mixing together literal truths about herself with lies and other people's dreams Acker has created a personal textual analog to the late 20th-century information crisis. Her texts blur time and space, skipping from 18th-century France to 20th-century hotel rooms, splicing gender and sexuality. Acker's are the kind of books that change those who read them. You've been warned.

Also recommended: My Mother: Demonology; Hannibal Lecter, My Father; In Memoriam to Identity; Empire of the Senseless; Blood and Guts in High School

The Atrocity Exhibition

by J.G. Ballard

1990; 127 pp.

$14 ppd (CA residents add sales tax) from: Re/Search, 20 Romolo St., Ste. B, San Francisco, CA 94133

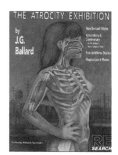

Originally published in 1969, **The Atrocity Exhibition** is both J.G. Ballard's most experimental, and most notorious work.

Told in a fragmented series of "compressed novels" (stories that have the density of a novel, but stripped of extraneous details like plot and characterization), **The Atrocity Exhibition** reads like the reports of a diseased medical clerk. It is the story of the mental breakdown of a psychiatrist bombarded by both his own obsessions and those of his patients, as they are all saturated by the cloud of media images coming in from all over the planet.

This new edition comes with stunning artwork by medical illustrator Phoebe Gloeckner, as well as four new stories, notes and annotations by Ballard himself. A work of high poetry and weird medical reportage, this is must reading for the end of the century.

Also recommended: **Crash**; **The Kindness of Women**; **Myths of the Near Future**; **War Fever**; **Concrete Island**; **The Crystal World**; **High-Rise**

Waiting for the End of the World

by Madison Smartt Bell

$9.95; Viking Penguin

1986; 324 pp.

Madison Smartt Bell's fiction describes a universe where broken people are trying to put themselves back together again—or destroy themselves utterly; sometimes they're doing both at the same time. In **Waiting for the End of the World** a group of minor league revolutionaries gets hold of some fissionable material and decides to blow up Manhattan as a grand terrorist act. Most of the book is devoted to the backgrounds of these men, losers all, and what happened to twist them into such a shape that destroying a city makes sense. This is where Bell soars. The combination of his white heat prose and eye for detail makes **Waiting for the End of the World**

fantastic without being fantasy, realistic without lapsing into social realism. He fuses the everyday world of filthy streets and lurching winos with bottomless horror, minor miracles and extraordinary sights. Eventually you realize that probably not far from you, are people whose lives and minds are so extravagant or so damaged or so *other* that blowing up a city seems like a perfectly reasonable way out.

Also recommended: **Dr. Sleep; The Year of Silence; The Washington Square Ensemble; Zero db and Other Stories**

Herotica

edited by Susie Bright

1988; 150 pp.

$12 ppd (CA residents add sales tax) from: Sexuality Library, 1210 Mission St., San Francisco, CA 94110

In **Herotica**, Susie Bright has collected an assortment of wonderfully erotic women's stories. There is something for every woman: gay, straight, or bisexual; kinky or cautious. As Bright writes in her introduction, "Some women want the stars, some the sleaze."

The situations range from the ordinary (a woman who meets a man in an art gallery, a weekend affair with a younger lover) to the fantastic (a science fiction tale of a planet where women initiate sex and men eagerly serve, a ghost story in which a woman has a rendezvous with a long-dead lover).

Many of the stories are playful and gently humorous, refusing to take their subject matter too seriously. But there is a feminine power in the honesty of the stories. The women in **Herotica** are aware of and willing to express their own sexuality. Sometimes, that means taking control of a situation; sometimes, being led by a lover. But always it means accepting and enjoying the sexual impulse. —Pat Murphy

Also recommended: **Herotica 2; Herotica 3**

The Terrible Girls

by Rebecca Brown
$8.95; City Lights
1990; 136 pp.

These are razor-sharp love stories that cut like a knife. They are almost too honest, too personal, too close to the bone. In fiercely beautiful language, Brown tells tales of love between women, with its honesty and denial, secrecy and betrayal, lust and obsession.

The particulars are difficult to describe: a traveler falls in love with a native. Lost in the strangeness of unfamiliar customs, in the intricacies of love and language, the lovers struggle to decipher the meanings of their actions. Where is the country? Who are the people? Brown doesn't say, and frankly the facts don't matter. The stories flow like poetry, telling the truth vividly. —Mary Maxwell

Fools

by Pat Cadigan
$5.99; Bantam Spectra
1992; 299 pp.

The losing and assuming of different identities has been a constant theme in Pat Cadigan's work. The problem with identity juggling, however appealing the idea might be in the abstract, becomes clear all too quickly—where does *me* begin and the identity graft end?

The protagonist of Fools is Mersine. And Marva 1 and Marva 2. And Marceline and Marya. The variants of the core personality's identity shift in and out of focus in a series of memories and half-recollections as she tries to piece together who she is and what she's been doing. Mersine, it seems, is a brain cop working her way into a personality bootlegging operation. She's under deep cover when she discovers that the personality overlay she's using to fool the Bad Guys has its own, separate, agenda. From there events, and identities, get very complicated.

Cadigan is a writer of considerable power, adept at drawing sympathetic characters, and with a quick, black wit. Fools is a very good writer's best book yet.

Also recommended: **Dirty Work**; **Mindplayers**; **Synners**

Cigarette Boy

A Mock Machine Mock-Epic presented to the Mackert Corporation
by Darick Chamberlin
1992; 84 pp.
$15 ppd from: Darick Chamberlin, 1562 E. Olive Way, #402,
Seattle, WA 98102

Conceptual novels are not a new idea. The most recent big-time practitioners have been the French who tried to express their post-war ennui in books that seemed determined to produce states of almost suicidal boredom in readers so that they could vicariously live out fictional characters' world-weary pout-fests. It was the literary equivalent of choking on second-hand cigarette smoke.

As a conceptual novel, **Cigarette Boy** is an altogether different beast. Its form is a data dump, an unparagraphed transcription of a computer's stream-of-consciousness musings. Imagine a machine version of **Finnegan's Wake**. The text is physically beautiful, smart and engaging, and, like **Finnegan's Wake**, requires a fair amount of work from the reader.

If you've ever had a computer do something so unexpected that it left you wondering "Why did you do that?" I'd advise you to check out **Cigarette Boy**. The answer may be closer than you think.

Carmen Dog

by Carol Emshwiller
$9.95; Mercury House
1990; 161 pp.

The premise is simple: all of the women in the world are turning into animals and many of the animals are turning into women. The heroine of the novel is Pooch, formerly a pedigreed retriever. Her mistress has grown irritable, bites when provoked, and smells distinctly of the marsh—apparently enroute to becoming a snapping turtle. Pooch's relationship with her master has also become strained. When the snapping turtle bites the baby, Pooch runs away, taking the child with her, and embarks on a series of adventures. Incidentally, Pooch's ambition in life is to sing *Carmen*, and I will tell you this—the story has a happy ending.

This is a humorous and peculiar adventure story, with narrow escapes and heroic acts. Carol Emshwiller's short stories have been published in both literary magazines and in science fiction publications, but her writing defies categorization. If you've been feeling a little slow and conventional lately, this book will shake your mind loose and encourage the strangest new thoughts. —Pat Murphy

Also recommended: The Start of the End of It All

Sarah Canary

by Karen Joy Fowler
$5.99; Zebra Books
1991; 384 pp.

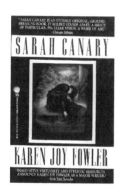

A woman friend once said to me, "I think woman are better than men at dealing with ambiguity." She may be right, at least in terms of fiction. Karen Joy Fowler's Sarah Canary is built on a series of ambiguities, mostly of perception. It begins with the title character, a seemingly mad woman who stumbles into a Chinese railworkers' camp in 1873. She cannot speak, but only makes sounds. To Chin, one of the Chinese workers (and a Mandarin scholar) she is most likely a goddess wandering the earth. To B.J., an asylum inmate who is unsure of his own existence, Sarah remains one of the shadows that haunt his life. To Adelaide, an early feminist lecturer, Sarah is a sister-in-the-cause. And Harold, a Civil War veteran who considers himself immortal because of his harrowing war years, sees in Sarah a fellow immortal.

Sarah herself is the ultimate ambiguity, utterly dependent on those who help her, but utterly free in her otherworldliness, her utter lack of interest in the rules of the world around her. The story and the lives the mysterious woman touches are caught in her vortex, finally to be flung out forever changed. This is a book about *aliens*, the ones who don't fit in. The world looks different through each pair of their eyes; their experiences have shown them different truths, and those are the truths they must live by.

Sarah Canary is funny and compelling, a historical novel that remains true to its period, but is very contemporary in its understanding of its characters, their lives and the ambiguities that make up any life.

Also recommended: Artificial Things

Virtual Light

by William Gibson
$21.95; Bantam Spectra
1993; 304 pp.

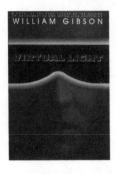

The sky above the port—you remember that from Neuromancer, don't you?—was the color of a television tuned to a dead channel... but a dead channel circa 1984—these days the color of a dead channel is quite likely a nice remarkable blue. On the first page of Virtual Light, the sky has turned to shit: "Fine flakes of fecal snow, billowing in from the sewage flats, have lodged in the lens of night." Virtual Light represents Gibson's return to the scene of the crime, dropping the other shoe, or what have you. It's the proper sequel to the Sprawl narratives; an Elmore Leonard novel on acid and a time machine.

The novel has two protagonists, both of whom are continuously more likable and more human than many earlier Gibson main characters. We meet Berry Rydell—ex-cop from Knoxville, Tennessee—in Los Angeles, where he is blindly continuing his career as a kind of strange attractor for the purest new millennium trouble. Then we go to San Francisco, where Chevette, a bike messenger who lives among wasp-hive dwellings plastered over the Bay Bridge, impulsively steals a set of self-contained virtual reality glasses that turn out to be the plot's Macguffin. Various folks—including San Francisco homicide cops who are native Russians and a semi-deranged hitman—chase after the glasses, and Rydell, attempting to recover from his latest catastrophe, is brought in to drive for one of the parties... well, you know, things happen.

Virtual Light continues Gibson's fascination with the technology that saturates our lives—from virtual reality glasses to voice-alarmed bicycles built from paper, to rent-a-cop vehicles that communicate with a satellite the vehicle's riders call the Death Star, to the latest Daihatsu with a hologram (defective, mind you) of a waterfall on its hood. Gibson presents not just the tech but the tech as experienced and rendered in tightly-focused presentations of sensory detail, and so makes it real, those imaginary gardens with real toads that Marianne Moore defined as poetry.

And that's the point, really: like all of Gibson's best work, Virtual Light creates a compelling and believable world in which even the most sordid, disgusting or violent phenomena are made beautiful by his prose. **Virtual Light** is prime Gibson work, not only beautiful but alarming and funny and violent. It gives kicks, but it's smart and has soul. —Tom Maddox

Also recommended: **Neuromancer**; **Count Zero**; **Mona Lisa Overdrive**; **Burning Chrome**; **The Difference Engine**

Gojiro

by Mark Jacobson
$5.99; Bantam Spectra
1991; 453 pp.

Many viewers of cheesy 60s Japanese giant-monsters-trashing-Tokyo flicks will recognize the name "Gojiro" as the original Japanese version of the name "Godzilla." Those viewers might also remember that many of those early movies featured a young boy, a sympathetic pal of Gojiro/Godzilla, whose presence and love proved that while the lizard might look and act like a homicidal flame-breathing hell beast, he was merely confused and misunderstood.

In Gojiro, Mark Jacobson takes seriously the idea of beast and human friend and marries it to one of the other themes of those early flicks—the A-Bomb. Remember that it was the Bomb that woke Gojiro from his long sleep and sent him stomping across the landscape. Gojiro was both the wrath of the Bomb and the Japanese spirit that was awakened by its fire. Jacobson manages to make the absurd premise of love between a monster and human not only work, but become touching as the boy is identified as a survivor, like Gojiro, of the Hiroshima blast.

By grabbing a handful of seemingly frivolous cultural icons and remixing them, with intelligence and respect for the power behind them, Jacobson has created a twistedly funny and touching novel.

Kalifornia

by Marc Laidlaw
$18.95; St. Martin's Press
1993; 245 pp.

Kalifornia is a ferociously entertaining trek through the proliferating underbrush of media domination. It's the next logical step in the progression that runs from Norman Spinrad's **Bug Jack Barron** through Paddy Chayefsky's *Network*. As modern media made each of those cautionary entertainments depressingly true, the fictional power needed boosting. I wonder how long until Marc Laidlaw's vision becomes the norm?

The book opens with the birth of the title character, a wired baby. The Figueroa family is the most famous family on the wires. They are quite literally wired, with an extra network implanted alongside their bodies' nervous systems. They transmit their every sensory impression, up to but not including their thoughts, over the network to a similarly wired population that not-so-vicariously experiences them. The birth of the baby Kalifornia is seen as a last ditch effort at saving the family's sagging ratings.

Laidlaw's future is wickedly funny, a *piñata* of wonders, cracked open and falling in delirious profusion across the pages. It would be easy for Laidlaw to have written this novel with a viciously mordant edge, as did Spinrad and Chayefsky before him, but he has instead written a genuinely heartfelt book populated with complex and mostly sympathetic characters. —Stephen P. Brown

Also recommended: **Dad's Nuke**; **Neon Lotus**

Easy Travel to Other Planets

by Ted Mooney
$10; Random House
1981; 240 pp.

This is one of the first novels that defined the idea of "slipstream" fiction. It's a beautiful evocation of everyday life—the uneasy truces and alliances with parents, the mysteries of sex and trust, the fear of the unknown—crossed with science fictional concerns—interspecies communication, future wars and "information sickness." The book's central character is Melissa, marine biologist. Her mother is dying of

cancer; her best friend is abused by her musician boyfriend. Her husband may be going off to Antarctica to report on a potential war. And Peter, the dolphin with whom Melissa has been working in a communication experiment, has recently become her lover. Mooney weaves the twisting lines of these lives together, moving effortlessly from character to character, male to female, even giving the dolphin a chance to tell a central story in his species' mythology, creating a fictional portrait of our times that feels more real than any realist novel could.

Also recommended: Traffic and Laughter

The Gold Bug Variations

by Richard Powers
$13; Harper Perennial
1991; 639 pp.

Who made us? Why? What's the purpose of life? It's all here. Profundities abound. Complications ensue.

The plot of The Gold Bug Variations is simple enough: Janet O'Deigh, a 29-year old Brooklyn librarian and her boyfriend, Franklin Todd, investigate the life of Stuart Ressler, an anonymous programmer who works the graveyard shift for a computer network. What befell Ressler, a once brilliant young geneticist on the fast track to the Nobel Prize? Jan and Franklin trace his disappearance, fall in love themselves, and befriend him. We are pulled deep into the world of molecular biology, the history of science and two love stories. The human relationships move through time in patterns that reflect the implications of the book's scientific speculation, i.e., are we the by-product of a formula for life? The title of the novel relates Poe's short story "The Gold Bug" and Bach's "Goldberg Variations" to a computer bug—the enigmatic variable at the heart of every code. The characters, too, form a double helix; the accumulation of relevant but finite details in a text of endless variety opens our consciousness to frightening scenarios and insistent echoes.

Richard Powers' two previous novels were also fueled by the interactions among science, research and history, but The Gold Bug Variations is his best-realized piece of work, and one of the most ambitious, original novels of recent years. —Leland Neville

Also recommended: Prisoner's Dilemma

....

Transreal!

by Rudy Rucker

1991; 535 pp.

$18 ppd (CA residents add sales tax) from: Mark V. Ziesing, P.O. Box 76, Shingletown, CA 96088; 916-474-1580

Rudy Rucker is:
a) a writer
b) a mathematician
c) a hacker
d) a sometimes worrying force of nature
e) all of the above

The answer is, of course, any, all of the above and more. Rudy's mathematics training has led him to study logic and higher dimensions that can only be expressed in numbers. A restless mind like that, that has seen numbers line up to create other realities, isn't likely to stay in one place very long. **Transreal!** is the first collection of Rudy's work that comes close to really showing what the inside of his skull looks like. His distinctive science fiction dominates the **Transreal!** terrain. Imagine Hunter Thompson on a surfboard, gobbling tabs of acid and spitting out quadratic equations. The book also contains his essays on everything from his first peek at a live sex show in New York to a run-in he had with Jerry Falwell to a field report from the trenches of Silicon Valley. The most revealing and surprising section of **Transreal!** is the first, a collection of poems from his college days, published before only in a minuscule print-run Xerox-chapbook form. In the poems you can see Rudy the writer in brittle chrysalis stage; other Rudys emerge in the text: Rudy the father, the student, the husband, a guy who has seen other worlds in numbers and wonders how to use that vision in his daily life. If you can't hack the math to get where Rudy's been, **Transreal!** is the next best way to get there.

Also recommended: **The Hollow Earth; Master of Space and Time; Spacetime Donuts; The Sex Sphere; Software; Wetware**

Glimpses

by Lewis Shiner

$21; William Morrow & Co.

1993; 320 pp.

A moody, melancholy novel of music, madness and time-travel. Ray Shackleford, a failed musician, discovers that he can record the "lost classics" of rock (i.e., would-be masterpieces that came within inches of being made) by closely visualizing the ideal circumstances of their recording. This ability, triggered by the death of his hated father, pulls him into a debilitating spiral of astral encounters with rock legends in alternate worlds where he attempts to help the artists create their fully-realized masterpieces: Jim Morrison's *Celebration of the Lizard*, Brian Wilson's *Smile*, Jimi Hendrix's *First Rays of the New Rising Sun*. In other words, while realizing how rock derives much of its rebellious power from fucked-up father/son relationships, Ray attempts to deal with his grief by altering musical history. This guy is into *massive* denial. But as Brian Wilson says, "God is in the music, man, and God *is* the father."

Ray finds healing eventually. At the center of the book is any fan's desperate prayer here (for Ray) finally requited: "If my idol only knew me, I'm sure we would be great friends." Such rampant wish-fulfillment requires more than a touch of "The Monkey's Paw" to give it an edge, and the book burns like a long, slow fuse. It has the power of Shiner's best short work, reading almost like a sustained version of the classic tale, "Jeff Beck," and evoking those aching feelings of anguish and loss that are such a huge part of rock's romance.
—Marc Laidlaw

Also recommended: **Frontera**; **Deserted Cities of the Heart**; **Slam**

New Noir

by John Shirley

1993; 115 pp.

$10 ppd from: The Talman Company, Inc., 131 Spring Street, #201E-N, New York, NY 10012; 800-537-8894

John Shirley is the author of dozens of stories and novels. His work—science fiction, horror, action, espionage—is characterized by a biting, surreal edge that instantly sets it apart from the mainstream. New Noir is a mix of streetlife with fantastic, hyperreal imagery—Borges as directed by Scorsese. The stories in this collection have a haunted quality. Like the streets of any big city, they are defined not by what's right in front of you, but by what's reflected in liquor store windows, encoded in the graffiti on abandoned cars. New Noir documents those slices of life you mostly don't see head-on, but catch quickly out of the corner of your eye.

Globalhead

by Bruce Sterling

1992; 301 pp.

$32.95 ppd (CA residents add sales tax) from: Mark V. Ziesing, P.O. Box 76, Shingletown, CA 96088; 916-474-1580

Bruce Sterling is known widely as the Chairman Mao of cyberpunk, at once the chief architect of its ideology and its reluctant wirehead-totem, wheeled out from his lab on State occasions to reassure the True Digital Believers that the dream (or simulation) is still alive... Sterling's intellectual restlessness has led him to experiment with a wide variety of story forms, many of which are collected in Globalhead; the tales range from a future history flashback in the form of a stodgy book review to a collaboration with Rudy Rucker in the gonzo UFO hunt, "Storming the Cosmos," to perhaps Sterling's best story to date, "We See Things Differently," a subtle tale of rock and roll, politics, war and belief told from the point of view of an intelligent and sympathetic Islamic terrorist.

Also recommended: Schismatrix; Islands in the Net; The Difference Engine; Mirrorshades

The Tangerine Tango Equation

By Barry Targan

$19.95; Thunder's Mouth Press
1990; 313 pp.

Nick Burden, the protagonist of **The Tangerine Tango Equation** is a genius; in fact, he has the highest IQ ever recorded. And unlike most geniuses, Nick is a polymath, meaning that he can aim his brain at pretty much any subject and suck it dry in a matter of weeks. If motivated, Nick might be able to find a cure for cancer or turn physics, and everything we know about the universe, upside down. As he enters college at the start of the novel, Nick's professors can't help but see him as an E ticket to a Nobel Prize. Nick's entrepreneurial roommate sees him both as a trustworthy associate and great cover for his shady business ventures. Reporters and teachers want to ride his coattails to fame. And throughout all this, while he wrestles with the fundamental laws of creation, Nick tries to come to grips with who and what he is: a universal thinking machine or a human being?

Elvissey

by Jack Womack

$12.95; Tor Books
1993; 334 pp.

Jack Womack's bent series plays off ideas about history, language, the machinations of capitalism and belief. In his earlier books icons such as Christ and Joseph Stalin had been reinvented in a corporate-dominated near future as cardboard advertising stand-ins, good for moving corn flakes and beer nuts, but nothing more. In **Elvissey**, though, it's the construction of a myth figure that dominates, or, at least, the attempted construction. Elvis, the charismatic ex-truck driver who shook up a few million libidos in *our* 1950s is to be kidnapped from a parallel 1950s where slavery never ended and where the alternate Elvis is, unfortunately, tone deaf and a killer.

Despite Womack's games with language and his twisted scenarios, **Elvissey** is a deeply felt and human book. Womack remains one of the few writers around who gets better and better with every book.

Also recommended: **Ambient**; **Terraplane**; **Heathern**

Witnesses from the Grave

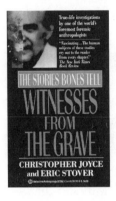

(The Stories Bones Tell)
by Christopher Joyce & Eric Stover
$4.99; Ballantine Books
1991; 322 pp.

A slick, but fascinating account of the life and work of forensic anthropologist, Clyde Snow. What's a forensic anthropologist? In Snow's case, he's an anthropologist who sifts through the evidence left by dead bodies—sometimes just bones and teeth—to determine both the identity of the body and, if possible, the cause of death. Snow's career has taken him from the Little Big Horn (where his findings partially rewrote the story of that battle) to Brazil where he examined a body identified as

Composite of exhumed skull with photo of Mengele; the match is perfect.

the remains of everyone's favorite missing Nazi, Josef Mengele, to Argentina where he worked alongside local teams identifying the corpses of civilians "disappeared" by the military.

Snow's cases are fascinating mystery stories, built on the kind of detail that makes for compelling fiction; the difference is that in Witnesses from the Grave, the stories are all true.

Pure Cop

by Connie Fletcher
$22.50; Villard Books
1991; 278 pp.

In What Cops Know, Fletcher let street cops tell their own stories—what it's like to work on the streets and how it effects their lives. Her new book, Pure Cop, does the same thing for police specialized units: the bomb squad, arson investigation, crime scene investigations, and hostage negotiations. By letting them speak for themselves, you get a clear look into the hearts and minds of these cops and their violent, unpredictable world.

Also recommended: What Cops Know

• *Criminals are the easiest of all hostage-takers to deal with. This idea of the desperate criminal is all wrong. Criminals are very logical people. They're logical. They're businessmen. They're out there sticking up; they're making money. They've invested their $35 for a pistol and they're gonna go out and make a 5000 percent profit. But it turns sour. The police have come; they've been frustrated in their escape, so they take this hostage so the police won't get them.*

Criminals go through two stages in these things: First come the demands for escape and then come the demands for survival.

You just let enough time go by where all of a sudden the light goes off over their heads—"Hey, they're not letting me out of here. They're gonna kill me." And then, if you can assure him he won't be hurt, he'll surrender.

World Encyclopedia of 20th Century Murder

by Jay Robert Nash

$49.95; M. Evans and Co.
1992; 693 pp.

Bloodletters and Badmen

by Jay Robert Nash

$17.95; M. Evans and Co.
1991; 640 pp.

Here they are—the crime buff's dream and the paranoid's wish list. Two books, over 1300 oversized pages, including bios and photos, of virtually every killer, tough guy and murderous babe that counts. While The World Encylopedia is a murderers-only club, Bloodletters and Badmen is sort of a capsule history of American crime, giving you the exploits of not only killers, but train robbers, cattle rustlers, mobsters and bandits from the 18th century to the present. Bon appetit!

Also recommended: Encyclopedia of World Crime

Serial Slaughter

by Michael Newton

1992; 173 pp.

$23.95 ppd (WA residents add sales tax) from: Loompanics Unlimited, P.O. Box 1197, Port Townsend, WA 98368

Between TV, movies and books, we've been treated to the antics of chainsaw killers, Hannibal the Cannibal, Ed Gein, Henry, the Boston Strangler and dozens of other junior varsity serial killers. But what does the inside of a real serial killer's mind look like? Where do they come from? Where do they hunt for their victims, and why? After studying the files of more than 800 serial killers, author Michael Newton answers many of these questions and even goes on to propose some possible cures for a situation that in the United Sates, at least, continues to grow every year.

Also recommended: **Hunting Humans**

- *The FBI sampling also reveals that 81% of the sex-killers surveyed were stimulated by pornography, beginning in childhood, but a cautionary note is necessary here. The anti-pornography crusade got a shot in the arm from Ted Bundy's eleventh-hour confessions, in February 1989— and crusader James Dobson reportedly banked $1 million hawking videotapes of the Bundy sermonette—but there are risks involved with taking such statements at face value. Bundy biographer Ann Rule describes the Dobson tape as "another Ted Bundy manipulation of our minds. The effect of the tape is to place, once again, the onus of his crimes—not on himself—but on us." It is also worth noting that Bundy's definition of "soft-core pornography" included pulp detective magazines, replete with crime photos and staged "jeopardy" scenes which also fueled the masturbatory fantasies of killers Eddie Cole and John Joubert. It comes as no surprise that rape-slayers enjoy pornography, but that enjoyment does not brand any given magazine or film as a "cause" of violent crime. Strangler Earle Nelson apparently limited his reading matter to the Holy Bible, and Heinrich Pommerenke killed his first victim after a viewing of The Ten Commandments convinced him women were the root of all evil.*

Whoever Fights Monsters

(My Twenty Years Hunting Serial Killers for the FBI)
by Robert K. Ressler & Tom Shachtman

$22.95; St. Martin's Press
1992; 256 pp.

Robert Ressler is the FBI agent who not only coined the term "serial killer," but also pioneered the use of psychological profiles to help catch them. In **Whoever Fights Monsters** he describes his 20-year career in the FBI and gives you an insider's look at cases in which he used psychological profiles to help lead police to murderers. He also recounts his face-to-face meetings with dozens of convicted killers, including Jeffrey Dahmer, John Wayne Gacy, Ed Kemper and David "Son of Sam" Berkowitz. This is a fascinating and unsensational book about a much-too-sensationalized subject.

- *Berkowitz told me that on the nights when he couldn't find a proper victim or proper circumstances, he would drive back to the scenes of earlier murders he had committed and revel in the experience of being where he had formerly accomplished a shooting....Seated in his car, he would often contemplate these grisly mementos and masturbate.*

  In this single moment of revelation, almost casually given, Berkowitz told us something extremely important for law enforcement, and at the same time provided new understanding to a staple of detective stories. Yes, murders did indeed return to the scene of their crimes, and we could try to catch future murderers on that basis. Equally as important, the world could now understand that this return to the scene of the crime arose not out of guilt, which had been the usual explanation accepted by psychiatrists and mental-health professionals, but because of the sexual nature of the murder. Returning to the murder site took on a connotation that Sherlock Holmes, Hercule Poirot, or even Sam Spade had never dared to suggest.

John Hinckley poses in front of Ford's Theater shortly before shooting President Reagan.

The Great American Medicine Show

by David Armstrong & Elizabeth Metzger Armstrong

$18; Prentice Hall
1991; 292 pp.

The next time you complain about the FDA's snail-like attitude toward approving new drugs, take a look at this book and be reminded that in the good old days anybody with a pill or a foul liquid, a crank belief, or just a good line of patter could market cures for everything from cancer to madness. Some of these healers had medical training and some were "layers on of hands." Dr. Benjamin Rush treated an ailing George Washington with his mercury powder, skin blistering and bleeding regimen, and croaked our first president. On the other hand, J.I. Rodale campaigned loudly against pesticides and chemical fertilizers in farming back in the early 1940s.

The Great American Medicine Show has them all, the lunatics and the visionaries, the militant vegetarians and the phrenologists, the electric-treatment boys who wanted to

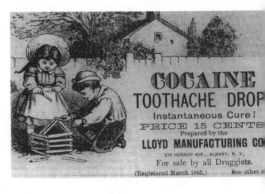

zap you back to health, and the bran fiends who had earthier ideas. You'll wonder how we ever managed to survive them all.

Psychedelics Encyclopedia

(Third Expanded Edition)
By Peter Stafford

$24.95; Ronin Publishing
1992; 420 pp.

A treat for the novice, the curious and the "experienced" alike, the Psychedelics Encyclopedia is part history lesson, part chemistry lesson and an even-handed examination of a class of drugs vilified by some and exalted by others.

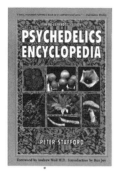

While a majority of this book is dedicated to the more widely known psychedelics such as LSD, mushrooms and mescaline, attention is also given to some of the substances more associated with shamanic traditions such as *ayahuasca, yagé* and Ibogaine.

This new updated edition includes reviews of the latest happenings in psychedelic research and culture, including the continued interest in psychedelics through the 80s into the 90s and the popularity of MDMA, ketamine and other compounds not so widely understood at the time of the first printing. —Mark Faigenbaum

- *The action of LSD is difficult to classify because it isn't specific, like aspirin or Miltown. More confusing, it also has variable effects at different dosages....Most users are affected by dosages above about 20 mcg. Amounts just above this produce effects somewhat like a long-lasting "hash-high;" Hoffman's initial trip is a fair example. From about 75 mcg. up to about 125 mcg., the amount usually taken, LSD can emphasize internal phenomena....A heavy dose—on the order of 200-250 mcg.—produces predominantly interior, revelatory experience. Higher doses tend to intensify the trip rather than lengthen it; above 400-500 mcg., there seems to be a "saturation point," beyond which increases make little difference.*

History Ends in Green

(Gaia, Psychedelics and the Archaic Revival)
by Terence McKenna

$43.95 (6 audio cassettes) ppd from: Mystic Fire Video,
 225 Lafayette St., #1206, New York, NY 10012; 800-292-9001

Terence McKenna, sometimes facilely referred to as "the Timothy Leary of the 90s," is a storyteller, a visionary, an eccentric and a believer in the power of psychedelic drugs to change human consciousness. **History Ends in Green** is a set of his talks on audio cassette, seven and a half hours altogether, in which he touches on not only the power of psychedelic experience, but evolution, spiritual transformation, the development of a global perspective and the importance of exploring both inner and outer space.

Part shaman, part sleight-of-hand man, McKenna embodies the qualities of the Trickster, the entity that tells you stories, sometimes true, sometimes not, that lead you to a new knowledge of yourself and the world.

Literary Outlaw

(The Life and Times of William S. Burroughs)
by Ted Morgan
$12.95; Avon Books
1988; 659 pp.

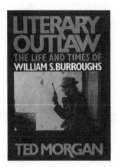

There are way too many biographies in the world today, especially biographies of artists. The fact is that most artists, and writers especially, spend a lot of time alone in rooms diddling. They write a sentence, toss it out. Write a page, kill half of it. Twist their own words around (or cut them up, in Burroughs' case) to see what they look like. Artists are self-absorbed and often, outside of their work, just aren't that interesting.

Burroughs hunting yagé in the Colombian jungle, 1953.

There are exceptions, however, and William Burroughs is one. His infamous William Tell episode with his wife has now been immortalized in film, but there's more than even that. Despite the sedentary nature of junkies, Burroughs' life has been lived in constant motion; he's lived all over the world, trying to find the perfect locale, where the rooms and boys were cheap and appealing, trying to stretch his meager trustfund dollars. He's hung out with everyone from Jean Genet to Chögyam Trungpa Rinpoche to Mick Jagger. And he's written a body of work that is inspiring a second and third generation of writers and visual artists.

Burroughs' prodigious drug use has reached legendary dimensions, and Morgan doesn't shy away from the subject. How could he? Drugs, as metaphor for transformation and as control system, are perhaps Burroughs' chief topic. If you haven't read Naked Lunch, do so immediately, and then read Literary Outlaw; you'll realize that everything in the first book was true, and everything in the second is an extension of the first.

PIHKAL

(A Chemical Love Story)
by Alexander Shulgin & Ann Shulgin
$18.95; Transform Press
1991; 978 pp.

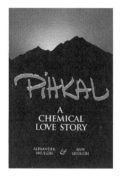

Alexander Shulgin is a well-respected chemist and an avid explorer. Not an explorer in the conventional sense, Shulgin journeys inward, towards the "interior universe."

In more than 30 years as a chemist, researcher and educator, he has synthesized over 200 hallucinogenic compounds and tested them on himself, his friends and his wife. Convinced of their value as tools to unlock and study the human psyche, Shulgin and his wife Ann share with the reader their experiences and journeys through chemical discovery. Journeys both hair-raising and deeply touching.

While the first half of the book is given over to personal experiences, the second half is a compendium of Shulgin's work, with 179 chemical formulas for hallucinogenic compounds he has synthesized, and brief notes about each one. Oh yes, it also really is a love story with Ann recounting the story of how she and Alexander met and came together, and the role that his compounds played in their becoming a couple. —Mark Faigenbaum

- *"I can't speak for other chemists, but I know that when I'm working in the lab, putting together a new compound, I not only see it upside down, inside out and in three dimensions, in my mind, but I also sense other aspects of what is developing. You might say that a personality or, to use your term, an entity, begins to takes shape as I work. I try to feel it out, to get a sense of whether it's friendly or not, whether it's liable to open up this area of the mind or that; does it have a dark nature which may mean I'm going to have to watch out for over-stimulation of the nervous system, or some other difficulty I can't anticipate? I can say, without any hesitation at all, that every compound I've discovered and tried has a real character all its own, quite as distinct as anything supposedly attached to a growing plant."*

SCUM Manifesto

by Valerie Solonas; 1968; 24 pp.

$3.95 ppd (CA residents add sales tax) from: AMOK Books, 1764 N. Vermont Ave., Los Angeles, CA 90027; 213-665-0956

In 1968, Valerie Solonas shot Andy Warhol. Too bad Andy hadn't read Valerie's recently printed political pamphlet; if he had, he might have known it was time to duck and cover.

The SCUM in the title is an acronym for the Society for Cutting Up Men. In her manifesto, Valerie concentrated her explosive rage against all males into one concentrated verbal blast. Of course, no one took her seriously. But then she plugged Warhol, proving herself a serious political theorist willing to act on her beliefs!

• *Life in this society being, at best, an utter bore and no aspect of society being at all relevant to women, there remains to civic-minded, responsible, thrill-seeking females only to overthrow the government, eliminate the money system, institute complete automation and destroy the male sex. But SCUM is impatient; SCUM is not consoled by the thought that future generations will thrive; SCUM wants to grab some thrilling living for itself. And, if a large majority of women were SCUM, they could acquire complete control of this country within a few weeks simply by withdrawing from the labor force, thereby paralyzing the entire nation. Additional measures, any one of which would be sufficient to completely disrupt the economy and everything else, would be for women to declare themselves off the money system, stop buying, just loot and simply refuse to obey all laws they don't care to obey. The police force, National Guard, Army, Navy and Marines combined couldn't squelch a rebellion of over half the population, particularly when it's made up of people they are utterly helpless without.*

The Abolition of Work

by Bob Black; 1986; 159 pp.

$13.95 ppd (WA residents add sales tax) from: Loompanics Unlimited, P.O. Box 1197,Port Townsend, WA 98368

The title of this collection of essays tells you exactly where Bob Black stands, and he isn't kidding. No friend to any established political group, including libertarian, anarchist, Marxist or conservative,

THE ABOLITION OF WORK

and other essays

BY BOB BLACK

Black is closest in spirit to André Breton and the Surrealists of the 20s. Like the original "Surrealist Manifesto," Black lays down, in the title essay of this book, the groundwork for the complete overthrow of everyday life.

Also included are such notable works as "A Lunatic Fringe Credo," "Feminism as Fascism," and "Anarchism and Other Impediments to Anarchy."

- *Socrates said that manual laborers make bad friends and bad citizens because they have no time to fulfill the responsibilities of friendship and citizenship. He was right. Because of work, no matter what we do we keep looking at our watches. The only thing "free" about so-called free time is that it doesn't cost the boss anything. Free time is mostly devoted to getting ready for work, going to work, returning from work, and recovering from work. No wonder Edward G. Robinson in one of his gangster movies exclaimed, "Work is for saps!"*

Better Dead Than Red

by Michael Barson
$12.95; Hyperion
1992; 143 pp.

A grim and hilarious look back at the good old days of red baiting, black lists and para-noia during the heyday of the Evil Empire. This copiously illus-trated book contains the best of the news world: J. Edgar Hoover and his commie-smashers, our on-again, off-again romance with Russia and Uncle Joe in particular, the smearing of Paul Robeson and Cuba-era air raid drills. The high art of the period isn't neglect-ed either, as we get plot summaries and publicity shots from such screen gems as *I Married a Communist*, *The Red Menace* and *Invasion, U.S.A.* Whenever you get nostalgic for the good old days "when things were simpler," pull **Better Dead Than Red** off the shelf and get a load of how cultural simplicity *really* looks.

T.A.Z.

(The Temporary Autonomous Zone, Ontological Anarchy, Poetic Terrorism)
by Hakim Bey; 1985; 141 pp.

$10 ppd (WA residents add sales tax) from: Loompanics Unlimited, P.O. Box 1197, Port Townsend, WA 98368

If Bob Black unfolds the roadmap to a Brave And Weirder New World in **The Abolition of Work**, then Hakim Bey is the guy who drives the welcome wagon. **T.A.Z.** is Groucho Marx's Freedonia, with fucking. It's where Dionysus caters everyone's birthday party. It's the place where Art won. Not Art as in something you see in field trips and art galleries, but Art as in demanding and living a miraculous life.

This book is a call to arms (or feet), a brick through the frosted glass of rationality.

* *Weird dancing in all-night computer-banking lobbies. Unauthorized pyrotechnic displays. Land-art, earthworks as bizarre alien artifacts strewn in State Parks. Burglarize houses but instead of stealing, leave Poetic-Terrorist objects. Kidnap someone & make them happy.*

  Pick someone at random & convince them they're heir to an enormous, useless & amazing fortune—say 5000 square miles of Antarctica, or an aging circus elephant, or an orphanage in Bombay, or a collection of alchemical mss. Later they will come to realize that for a few moments they believed in something extraordinary, & will perhaps be driven as a result to seek out some more intense mode of existence....

  Organize a strike at your school or workplace on the grounds that it does not satisfy your need for indolence and spiritual beauty.

Open Magazine Pamphlet Series

P.O. Box 2726
Westfield, NJ 07091
Individuals $30 (10 issues/year); Students $27

A series of beautifully produced and wonderfully provocative agit-prop pamphlets from such writers as Noam Chomsky, Mike Davis, Rosalyn Baxandall and Mark Dery, covering topics from Malcolm X to urban control, the Middle East to AIDS, from colonialism to abortion rights.

• From *Urban Control: The Ecology of Fear by Mike Davis: In contemporary metropolitan Los Angeles, a new species of special enclave is emerging in sympathetic synchronization to the militarization of the landscape. For want of a generic appellation, we might call them "social control districts" (SCDs). They merge the sanctions of the criminal or civil code with land-use planning to create what Michel* Foucault would have undoubtedly have recognized as further instances of the evolution of the "disciplinary order" of the twentieth-century city.

THE ECOLOGY OF FEAR

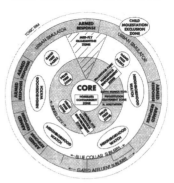

Davis' *Neuromancer*-inspired social map of a future L.A.

As Christian Boyer paraphrases Foucault: "Disciplinary control proceeds by distributing bodies in space, allocating each individual to a cellular partition, creating a functional space out of this analytic spatial arrangement. In the end this spatial matrix became both real and ideal: a hierarchical organization of cellular space and a purely ideal order that was imposed upon its forms...."

The obverse strategy, of course, is the formal exclusion of the homeless and other pariah groups from public spaces. Los Angeles and Pomona are emulating the small city of San Fernando (Ritchie Valens' hometown) in banning gang members from parks. The "Gang Free Parks" reinforce non-spatialized sanctions against gang membership as examples of "status criminalization" where group membership, even in the absence of a specific criminal act, has been outlawed.

Archives on Audio

P.O. Box 170023, San Francisco, CA 94117-0023; 415-346-1840

A collection of researcher and broadcaster Dave Emory's radio shows on cassette tapes. Topics include the INSLAW and Iran-Contra scandals, the CIA's drug connections, the Kennedy Assassination, Vietnam, Nazis employed by the U.S. government after WWII and other non-mainstream takes on politics. Tape prices range from $8 (with postage) to about $25. The catalog is free.

Ada, the Enchantress of Numbers

by Betty Alexandra Toole

$29.95 ppd from: Critical Connection, P.O. Box 452, Sausalito, CA 94966

Will somebody intelligent like Stanley Kubrick please make a great movie about Ada, Lady Lovelace? Daughter of Lord Byron, companion and partner to Charles Babbage, and history's first programmer, Ada was one of the most picturesque characters in the history of technology, and one of the great eyewitness historians of technology. When Babbage designed and built automatic calculating devices, Ada, a mathematical prodigy, grasped the essence of using mathematical operations to control the operations of the machine. Ada's letters are some of the classic founding documents of cybernetics and computer science, written nearly a century before ENIAC, the first electronic digital computer. The U.S. Defense department named its standard software language after her.

Ada, Lady Lovelace

Her life was colorful enough for Hollywood in the 1990s. Ada's friends included Dickens, Prince Albert, Wheatstone and Faraday. Biographers have depicted her struggles with morphine addiction, her weakness for literally gambling the family jewels on the ponies. She was a 21st-century woman in Victorian England, and most of what was written about her by others was colored by the way Ada went against the grain in an age when women who went against the grain were fed morphine tonic and put to bed. It may never be possible to sort out the myth and reality surrounding Ada. She did, however, leave an extensive correspondence.

The editor of this annotated collection of Ada's letters—including the historic description of Babbage's "Analytical Engine"—lets Lovelace speak for herself. —Howard Rheingold

Lipstick Traces

(A Secret History of the 20th Century)
by Greil Marcus

$14.95; Harvard University Press
1990; 516 pp.

Public school teaches us many lies, one of which is that history is the story of BIG EVENTS. Our lives, we are led to believe, are removed from the processes of history; we are tacitly taught that we live outside of history. We can see history on television (when it isn't censored); we can buy it in books and magazines, but we can't participate in it because our lives are simply too small.

But what if history doesn't function according to public school models? What if the small things—secret lives, dreams and obsessions—have a place in history? What if ordinary lives (ordinary in the sense that they have no access to real power) mattered in the shape of things?

In the mid-70s Greil Marcus, like many of us, heard an ordinary voice from England, a singer who couldn't sing, so he shouted. What he shouted was: "I AM AN ANTICHRIST!" The singer was Johnny Rotten, the band was the Sex Pistols, and the sound of that ragged, tuneless voice came to haunt Marcus.

The result of Rotten's shout and Marcus' obsession with it is a book, **Lipstick Traces**, subtitled "A Secret History of the 20th Century." Here Marcus begins with Rotten and moves backwards, looking for his antecedents, the other ordinary voices that, while not shaping national borders or inventing neurosurgery, left the world different. In Marcus' history class we don't hang with Thomas Jefferson or Mao, but teenage punks, French anarchists, Dadaists, even Christian mystics—people with small voices whose passion and occasional madness, Marcus contends, help determine the shape of the world we have come to inhabit.

Does Marcus' hypothesis hold up under scrutiny? Yes, for the most part, but that hardly matters. **Lipstick Traces** reclaims history from the history-writers, the history-makers—academics, generals flush with victory, politicians—and throws the steaming guts of the 20th century into the street—*plop!*—for the dogs and passersby to see the truth: that history is just people living their lives, trying to have a good time, hoping that in the end it all means something.

This isn't the history of rock and roll; this is history *as* rock and roll.

Guillotine

(Its Legend and Lore)
by Daniel Gerould
1992; 329 pp.
$16.95 ppd from: Blast Books, P.O. Box 51, Cooper Station, New York, NY 10276

If you missed the two-hundredth birthday of the guillotine (April, 1992), you can make up for it with this fine volume: **Guillotine, Its Legend and Lore.**

As French as croissants and the clap, the machine was originally designed as a humane way to execute prisoners condemned by the Revolutionary French National Assembly. Unfortunately, the guillotine proved too simple and easy to use, and while it probably did lessen the pain of individuals condemned to death, it created an assembly-line mentality that demanded more and more heads to feed the machine. While the meat was flying, a whole pop culture infrastructure grew up around the machine, complete with funny songs, political cartoons, guillotine toys and, later, cheesy films. It's this cultural aspect of the guillotine that's the focus of Daniel Gerould's well-researched and sometimes wickedly funny book.

Guillotining in France, 1902

• *Many nineteenth-century Americans on grand tours to Europe tried to take in at least one guillotining during their travels.... By 1853 the reductions of regional executioners in France led to the public auctioning of scaffolds and accessories in regions where they could no longer be of service. Often the wood was rotten and the metal rusty. Collectors began buying guillotines, and they began to show up at fairs as macabre attractions. Some executioners and their widows kept the machines, particularly the blades of supposedly "historic" guillotines, and later sold them to collectors at high prices. A number of blades "certified" to have decapitated Louis XVI were put up for sale over the years.*

The executioner became something of a social celebrity and tourist attraction.

The Trial of Gilles de Rais

by Georges Bataille

1991; 279 pp.

$16.45 ppd (CA residents add sales tax) from: AMOK Books, 1764 N. Vermont Ave., Los Angeles, CA 90027; 213-665-0956

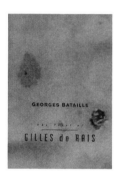

Gilles de Rais, lieutenant to Joan of Arc, soldier and aristocrat, was the model for the mythical murdered Bluebeard. By his own admission, on his return home after Joan of Arc's execution, he ritually slaughtered hundreds of local children for his own pleasure. Georges Bataille, a philosopher of the monstrous, dissects one of history's true monsters, looking not only for Gilles de Rais' motives, but for his analogs in our own time. This is an unsettling and riveting book, and especially timely at the end of the Cold War, when the U.S. is trying to redefine its role both as a nation and a military power.

The book also includes records of Gilles de Rais' actual trial, translated from the ecclesiastical Latin.

- *In Gilles de Rais' time, war was always the game of lords. If this game devastates populations, it exalts the privileged class. It has for the privileged class the ultimate meaning that work could never have for the poor folk. The interest of work is subordinated to its result; the interest of war is nothing but war. It is war itself which fascinates and which terrifies. Those who are like Gilles de Rais, who live in the expectation of these terrible battles leaving death, cries of horror, and suffering behind them, know nothing else that gives them this violent excitement. Present generations no longer know practically anything about the exaltation, even though death was the basis of it, that formerly was the least ridiculous meaning and aim of war, a fact that is likely to abandon us to a feeling of our powerlessness in the world. Are we not blinded when the mad truth of another time is hidden from us?*

PLACE ....

Equatoria

by Richard & Sally Price
$27.50; Routledge
1992; 295 pp.

Is it a new form of non-fiction, or simply a peculiar one? The Prices are a couple of teachers who, in 1990, went off to French Guiana to hunt down native crafts for a new museum. Along the way, they encountered many of the hardships and absurdities that always accompany adventures in the developing world, traveling up rivers to meet people who haven't exactly been waiting for you with bated breath. What makes this book different from others of its type are two things: one, the Prices begin to question, among other things, the value of collecting native objects and sticking them behind glass without context, and how displaying "primitive" art can create a kind of cultural power vacuum in which the developed world gets all gooey and paternalistic toward the amusing little brown people.

The second thing that makes Equatoria different is that the book is written in a kind of cinematic split-screen effect. The right hand page contains the Price's straightforward account of their buying trip in Guiana, while on the left hand page is a running commentary on the action. Sometimes the commentary is just a helpful illustration or a quote from other travelers they encountered in Guiana; more often than not, though, it's a sardonic quote (sardonic either in content or context) from writers like Swift, Conrad, Alex Haley, Márquez and Germaine Greer. This commentary utterly transforms the travel account on the opposite page, charging it with subtleties and hidden meanings usually lacking in even the best-intentioned works of the kind.

America

by Jean Baudrillard
$13.95; Verso
1986; 129 pp.

Meditations, critiques, theories and rants that read like the great novel Ballard never wrote. America as the desert of the imagination, an empty landscape waiting to be filled by the fantasies and dreams of a still young nation burdened and blessed with a restless, adolescent culture. Baudrillard's prose gleams like a piece of surgical equipment, or the chrome headlight mounts on a new Jaguar.

Also recommended: **Simulations, Fatal Strategies**

- *Irvine: a new Silicon Valley. Electronic factories have no openings to the outside world, like integrated circuits. A desert zone, given over to ions and electrons, a supra-human place, the product of inhuman decision-making. By a terrible twist of irony it just had to be here, in the hills of Irvine, that they shot "Planet of the Apes." But, on the lawn, the*

American squirrel tells us all is well, and that America is kind to animals, to itself, and to the rest of the world, and that in everyone's heart there is a slumbering squirrel. The whole Walt Disney philosophy eats out of your hand with these pretty little sentimental creatures in grey fur coats. For my own part, I believe that behind these smiling eyes there lurks a cold, ferocious beast fearfully stalking us.... On the same lawn with the squirrel stands a sign put there by some society of Jesus: "Vietnam, Cambodia, Lebanon, Grenada — We are a violent society in a violent world!"

Motoring with Mohammed

by Eric Hansen

$10; Vintage Departures
1991; 240 pp.

A storm at sea. A shipwreck. Ten years later, a traveler returns to find the notebooks and journals he buried on a miniscule island frequented only by smugglers and terrorists. It's not a Woody Allen movie, it's Eric Hansen's life. How he makes his way back through Yemen, and attempts to retrieve his lost notebooks, is entertaining and enlightening. A real-life tale of perseverance and absurdity.

The Sphinx in the City

(Urban Life, the Control of Disorder, and Women)
by Elizabeth Wilson
$14; University of California Press
1991; 191 pp.

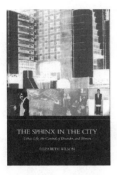

The "fateful pleasures" and "enormous anxieties" of modern cities as seen, specifically, from a woman's point of view. Elizabeth Wilson uses a blur of fiction, history, movies and art to peel away the layers of traditional description that surround some of the world's most famous cities: London, Paris, Moscow, São Paolo, and others. Wilson examines the promise of the city—freedom from traditional family roles and sexual freedom—as they're balanced by specifically urban dangers (muggers, rapists) and the kind of design and social barriers (fortress-mentality city centers) that keep *the others* at bay.

• *The contemporary urban woman is both consumer and consumed.... The ambivalence of her role was forcefully illustrated by the real-life tragedy of Suzy Lamplugh, who worked as an estate agent in London. At her place of work she was seated at a prominent position in the office window, so that her good looks would attract custom, yet she was expected to go out unaccompanied with male clients. When she disappeared, it was assumed that one of these male clients had murdered her: the mystery has never been solved. Her car, her experience, her streetwise knowledge, did not save her. In a curious way, her alleged sexual past was even used against her in the media story that was created. Women like Suzy Lamplugh embody the ambivalence of the postmodern city.*

Postmodern Geographies

by Edward Soja
$16.95; Verso
1989; 266 pp.

Writer and professor of urban planning, Edward Soja casts an unapologetically Marxist eye on the uses of space in contemporary cities. The control of space, who has access to space, what is seen and unseen from different spaces, are all, in Soja's view, questions and conditions of power. As Soja says in his combination

Preface/Postscript, "Today...it may be space more than time that hides consequences from us, the 'making of geography' more than the 'making of history' that provides the most revealing tactical and theoretical world."

Soja's essays aren't tidy bits of academe, but debates on the history and future of the urban landscape; like modern cities themselves, Soja's narratives are full of detours, sidetracks, congested intersections and unexpected imagery.

American Mythologies

by Marshall Blonsky

$30; Oxford University Press
1992; 517 pp.

Semiotics is the study of cultural artifacts to uncover their hidden "signs;" in other words, certain cultural objects hold more meaning than appears directly on the surface. I first understood this idea when traveling through rural Nepal and Thailand, I saw posters of Rambo and Madonna on the walls of mud huts. Blonsky's book traces the marks images like these leave in the cultural landscape of the world, letting us catch a glimpse of how the world sees us, and some of the hidden ways we see ourselves.

Safe in its sanctuary is vitamin-enhanced Barbie in the hands of new convert to capitalism, 6-year-old Anika Polzin of Schwenefeld, once East Germany. The end of her first day of shopping in Helmstedt, then West Germany. —from *American Mythologies*

War in the Age of Intelligent Machines

by Manuel De Landa

$16.95; MIT Press
1991; 271 pp.

Imagine a history of military technology and artificial intelligence written by a future robot historian seeking to explain the evolution of its kind. If you're thinking this sounds more like a science fiction novel than a serious non-fiction work, you're right, but that, explicitly, is what Manuel De Landa has set out to do and has done.

Moreover, he has applied some very difficult ideas taken from the French post-Structuralist Gille Deleuze and from chaos theory and used them as the framework on which to hang his exposition. In particular, the notion of the "machinic phylum," taken from Deleuze and defined as "...The overall set of self-organizing processes of the universe," serves as the primary concept that structures the book. De Landa uses the idea to explore the growth of military technology and, ultimately, the strange ground that we stand on today, where the lines have blurred separating military from civilian, organic from inorganic, life from non-life, intelligent from non-intelligent.

He takes the reader on a strange and demanding trip, rigorous in its discussion of technologies (such as fortification building or the development of the conoidal bullet) and adheres strictly to his abstract and often difficult conceptual framework. The result is a tough and peculiar and rewarding book, one that made me feel new wrinkles in my brain. —Tom Maddox

- *The efforts of military institutions to get humans out of the loop have been a major influence in the development of computer technology. The birth of autonomous weapons systems, of war games played by automata, of production systems that pace and discipline the worker, all are manifestations of this military drive. But...even though humans are being replaced by machines, the only schemes of control that can give robots the means to replace them...are producing another kind of independent "will" which may also "resist" military domination. For example, the future of the military depends on the correct functioning of its worldwide command and control networks, like the WWMCCS. This network, up to the 1970s, was designed around a centralized scheme of control (batch processing) that caused bottlenecks and delays, even when operating without the friction produced by war. To make a global command and control network a functional entity the military needed to replace a central computer handling the traffic of messages with a scheme where the messages themselves had the ability to find their own destination. The messages had to become demons.*

However, when demons are allowed to barter, bid and compete among themselves for resources, they begin to form "computational societies" which resemble natural ecologies (like an insect colony) or even human ecologies (like a marketplace). In other words, demons began to acquire a degree of independence from their designers.

Sell Yourself to Science

by Jim Hogshire

1992; 160 pp.

$20.95 ppd (WA residents add sales tax) from: Loompanics Unlimited, P.O. Box 1197, Port Townsend, WA 98368

Got an extra kidney you're not using? Maybe some bone marrow that's just sitting there, economically underutilized? Maybe you have some time on your hands and wouldn't mind field-testing a new drug for some pharmaceutical firm? Then step right up!

That's right kids, your body is an untapped gold mine of cells, fluids and experimental terrain. To learn how to get your piece of the sharecropping pie, all you need is Sell Yourself to Science. Who needs to give a pound of flesh when a pint of your rare blood-type will do?

• *Getting paid for jacking off is every teenage boy's dream. These days it's easier than ever to realize this elusive goal. Dozens of sperm banks are listed in Appendix Six. For more information on egg and sperm donation contact:*

Fertility Research Foundation
1430 Second Avenue, Suite 103
New York, NY 10021
(212) 744-5500

Simians, Cyborgs & Women

(The Reinvention of Nature)
by Donna Haraway
$16.95; Routledge
1991; 287 pp.

Simians, Cyborgs & Women is part essay, part autobiography, tracking the transformation of a "socialist-feminist, white, female, hominid biologist" into "a multiply marked cyborg feminist."

The essays focus on gender roles in scientific discovery, and on nature—its invention, mutation and reinvention in the late 20th century. The first third of the book describes the battleground of the natural world (as close as the body, and as far as the land); the middle section "explores contests for the power to determine stories about 'nature' and 'experience'—two of the most potent and ambiguous words in English."

It's in the third, fascinating section of the book that Haraway shines, and where she proves herself to be a true heretic. The centerpiece of the section is "A Cyborg Manifesto," a controlled and sustained brain-burn in which Haraway not only lays out the problems of *perspective* in a postmodern culture, but she actually offers a solution: what she calls "cyborg embodiment," a dual point of view formed from the psychic melding of the organic and the machine, forming a hybrid creature that slips easily between both natural and unnatural worlds. In "A Cyborg Manifesto," Haraway has constructed a Declaration of Independence for mutants, an anthem for a planet of bombarded and fragmented post-humans—the hopeful monsters who will hop and wobble their way across the minefield of postmodern culture into the next century and beyond. Utopia will never be the same.

- *By the late 20th century, our time, a mythic time, we are all chimeras, theorized and fabricated hybrids of machine and organism; in short, we are cyborgs. The cyborg is our ontology; it gives us our politics. The cyborg is a condensed image of both imagination and material reality, the two joined centers structuring any possibility of historical transformation. In the tradition of Western science and politics...the relation between organism and machine has been a border war. The stakes in the border war have been the territories of production, reproduction, and imagination. This...is an argument for pleasure in the confusion of boundaries and for responsibility in their construction."*

"...I would rather be a cyborg than a goddess."

Artificial Reality II

by Myron Krueger
$29.95; MIT Press
1991; 286 pp.

Jaron Lanier may get the big press when it comes to virtual reality, but Myron Krueger was there first, mapping out worlds, art and actions that could only take place inside a computer, a good decade before most of the world was paying attention. In 1975, he opened VIDEOPLACE, an interactive "laboratory" incorporating computer graphics, video and position-sensing devices. Artificial Reality II is an update of his visionary 1983 book, Artificial Reality. The book is more of a memoir of time spent in the computer mines than a catalog of dazzling superwonders to come, making it an unusually personal book on science and the possibilities of technology.

- *Although technology has failed to relieve tedium, it has all but eliminated physical labor from most jobs. However, because our bodies require physical exertion for health, we face the irony that doctors ask us to devote an hour to exercise after we get home from work. Since our labor-saving devices have in this sense lengthened rather than shortened our working day, we must find ways to reintroduce physical effort into our jobs, so that we can get paid while we satisfy this need.*

Trialogues at the Edge of the West

by Ralph Abraham, Terence McKenna & Rupert Sheldrake
1992; 175 pp.
$16.45 ppd from: Bear & Co., P.O. Drawer 2860, Santa Fe, NM 85904-2860; 800-932-3277

Discussions, arguments, rants and inspired riffing by three scientist/professional characters with a lot to say. Ralph Abraham is a mathematician and the godfather of chaos theory; Terence McKenna is a shamanologist and ethno-pharmacologist; and Rupert Sheldrake is a radical biologist and originator of the idea of "morphic resonance," a kind of memory that is embedded in all systems.

In a series of ten "trialogues" the three hash over everything from green consciousness to the nature of physical reality to how chaos impacts our daily lives to the Apocalypse, and beyond. Heady stuff from three major intellects unafraid of stepping on scientific toes and pushing the envelope of what we know.

Sexual Portraits

by Michael Rosen; 1990; 63 pp.

$27 ppd (CA residents add tax); illustrated brochure $1; both from:
Shaynew Press, P.O. Box 11719,
San Francisco, CA 94101

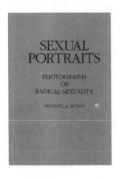

A sympathetic photo and interview book focusing on people who live and play outside the sexual mainstream: piercers, drag queens, dominants, submissives, and others. **Sexual Portraits** is frank, informative and erotic without ever being exploitive.

Books like this are dangerous because they can leave you reconsidering your own life....

Carla and Fakir Musafar, 1988

Also recommended:

Sexual Magic (The S/M Photographs)

Sex for Beginners

by Errol Selkirk

$7.95; Writers and Readers
1988; 221 pp.

Not a how-to manual. Not unless theories about sexuality turn you on. We have psychological and gender theories about sex; the Greeks on Eros, Sade on power, and Angela Carter on pornography; sex in the east and sex in the west; and, of course, highlights from Freud and Reich. The successful comic-book format of the "Beginners" series (Marx, Freud, **Zen for Beginners**, etc.) zips right along through these and other sexual historical climaxes to the concluding speculations on where the sexual revolution is leading us and the challenge of AIDS. (For over four centuries, contracting syphilis was the same as receiving a death sentence, the authors remind us.) Perspective is what this book is about— the cultural baggage that comes attached to each tasty kiss. *Smack.*
— Jeanne Carstensen

• *Sexual attitudes often reveal a great deal about the structures and values of a society. The people of Samoa, for example, never appreciated the merits of the Missionary Position. In their culture men and women were more equal than in Europe. Why, under these circumstances, should the female always be below? Besides, an islander might add, this position often hampers the woman with the weight of the man. Isn't it better that both parties stay active, so that each can give and get more pleasure?*

Susie Bright's Sexual Reality:

(A Virtual Sex World Reader)
by Susie Bright
$9.95; Cleis Press
1992; 157 pp.

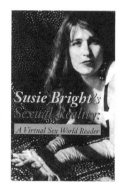

Who needs Dr. Ruth when we have Susie Bright? As a sex educator, theoretician and practitioner, Susie has few equals, combining humor and intelligence with her extensive, well, fieldwork on the subject of sexuality. One of the things that makes Susie special is that, although she's in the thick of lesbian politics, she's more interested in what people do than what they call themselves. Back when she edited the lesbian zine *On Our Backs*, she designed a survey that didn't allow readers to call themselves gay, bi or straight. They could only answer questions about how they had sex, and with whom. Her writings about sex and sexuality are personal and nakedly honest, full of fun facts to know and tell, and anecdotes that range from the funny to the painful. But that's Susie's virtual sex world, a life carnival, and you're all invited.

• *Masculinity in the nineties has been erotically revived and challenged from unexpected quarters: women and gays. A lot of heterosexual men find this ridiculous, offensive, and even amazing. After all, what does being a man have to do with girls and queers?*

A man is many things, not the least of which is his sexual style. The classic image of masculine sexiness requires handsome beauty, strength, a clear, steady gaze, and a bit of the devil. Anyone, regardless of sexual preference, can both appreciate and attain these qualities. While many heterosexual men take for granted the erotic presentation of masculinity, gay men have built a whole aesthetic upon it— first in gay pornography, then in mainstream popular culture. Who's to say what came first—the Honcho *centerfold or the Marlboro man?*

Love Bites

by Della Grace; 1991; 71 pp.

$33.45 ppd (CA residents add sales tax) from: The Sexuality Library, 1210 Mission St., San Francisco, CA 94110

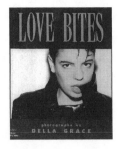

In **Love Bites**, photographer Della Grace flashes on the tough heart-beat of dykelife: posers, lovers, clubbers, gay rights marchers and S/M players. From San Francisco to London, Grace parts the pink leather curtain and gives us an erotic glimpse of life in the cool zone.

Grace, American-born and now brewing in London, is making big waves on both sides of the Atlantic as one of the most controversial and accomplished lesbian photographers around. Her punk-chic porn has steamed up the pages of *On Our Backs*, and has fueled fires in galleries from L.A. to Edinburgh. But Grace became truly notorious when **Love Bites** was briefly seized by American customs officials who cried obscenity during a moral temper tantrum.

Grace's style is sweet, yet streetwise. Her photos blend club scene fashion with gender-bending sex play, creating a document of the

new lesbian nation. Wrapped in wedding veils, chain mail, combat boots, or fishnet stockings, Grace's subjects of desire are women with a distinct look and purpose.

In the series titled "Ruff Sex," a blonde in a latex dress bends over for a cunt full of dildo, while another set of hands holds her golden dreadlocks in place. Hand-coloring on some of these black and white images casts a soft light on a rough scene, bringing beauty face to face with aggression. Other pieces, such as "Cold-Store Romance," are full-color, flash-filled visions of playful decadence. Against a night sky and a smear of graffiti, Robyn and Angie spin pink tutus while they stick their hands in dark places.

Love Bites fuses lesbian glamour with erotic identity to produce sexual portraits of women who are real powerhouses, not just pretty faces. —Lisa Palac

Sex Work

(Writings by Women in the Sex Industry)
ed. by Frederique Delacoste & Priscilla Alexander
$10.95; Cleis Press
1987; 349 pp.

This is a cutting-edge book on a virtually unexplored topic: sex workers as subject and not object. These include street prostitutes, call girls, porn actresses, massage parlor workers and others. The first-person stories that fill the first two-thirds of the book relate a wide variety of experiences in personal detail: a woman in her 50s who becomes a well-paid prostitute in Paris; another woman working in a massage parlor in San Francisco; a prostitute getting raped and trying to get help from the police in San Jose; a writer/call girl writing and working happily out of her home; a young girl's first time working the street in Berkeley. No attempt is made to generalize about why these women are sex workers; each story is raw and individual.

The last third of the book contains essays from international sex workers' groups like WHISPER (Women Hurt in Systems of Prostitution, Engaged in Revolt), The Red Thread ("The whores' movement in Holland") and COYOTE (Cast Off Your Old Tired Ethics). These organizations help sex workers achieve the safest working conditions possible and lobby for programs to help find them other work if they want it. For most groups this means decriminalizing prostitution. Priscilla Alexander's essay, "Prostitution: A Difficult Issue for Feminists," is an excellent historical overview of prostitution.

Also included is an extensive bibliography of books by and about prostitutes, fiction and non-fiction. — Jeanne Carstensen

Giger's Alien

by H.R. Giger

1979; 75 pp.

$45.45 ppd (CA residents add sales tax) from: Morpheus International, P.O. Box 7246, Beverly Hills, CA 90212-7246

Giger's long career of painting "biomechanical" images reached a public peak when he was asked to design the extraterrestrial sets and the monster for the film *Alien*. This book documents, through notes, photos, working sketches and full-scale paintings, the development of the basic alien design (inspired by one of Giger's own works), to its final gruesome form on film. The reproductions in this book are beautiful, clear and on excellent paper.

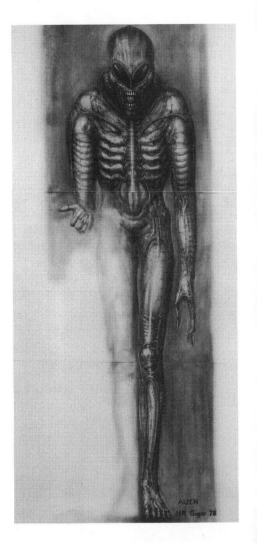

Morpheus International handles a whole range of Giger items, including his other books (H.R. Giger's Necronomicon, H.R. Giger's Biomechanics), high-quality prints that go for around $300 and posters for around $20. The Morpheus catalog is free.

Ecstatic Incisions

by Freddie Baer

1992; 73 pp.

$13.95 ppd (CA residents add sales tax) from: AK Distribution, P.O. Box 40682, San Francisco, CA 94140-0682

Freddie Baer slices and dices contemporary and Victorian imagery into vibratory eyeball snacks. Some of the work here is beautiful for beauty's sake, while some is highly political; all of it, to paraphrase Odilon Redon, places the conscious at the service of the unconscious.

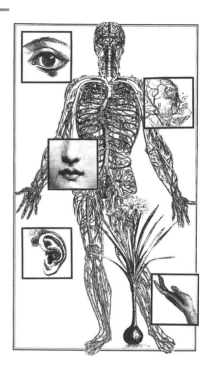

Diva Obsexion

ed. by R.M.-S.P.-F.d.Z.

1992; 104 pp.

50.000 Lire ppd (cash, bank check or international money order) from: Glittering Images edizioni d'Essai, Via Giovanni da Montorsoli, 37/39 50412 Firenze, Italy; tel/fax 055-717880

Each of the 12 Glittering Images "Diva" volumes looks at women in pop art: TV, books, and especially, movies and comics. Diva Obsexion concentrates on some of the more tasteful imagery found in S&M art, Women in Prison flicks, detective and crime pulp horror films and "photo comics" (see illo at right). The "Diva" series is like some weird and beautiful encyclopedia of the forbidden.

ART ....

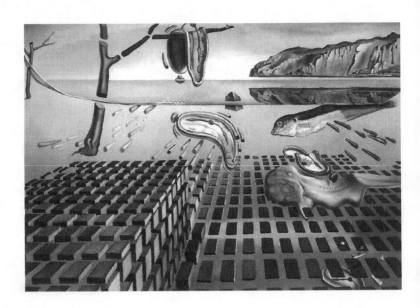

Salvador Dali Museum Catalog

catalog free from: Salvador Dali Museum, 1000 Third Street South, St. Petersburg, FL 33701; 813-823-3767; orders only 800-442-DALI

The largest collection of Salvador Dali's work outside Europe resides in a town known more for its heat and clever tourist trinkets, such as coconuts carved like monkeys. The museum is a wonder, however. If you don't plan on making it to Florida, the museum's free catalog has a load of high-quality Dali prints, silk-screened T-shirts, videos, recordings and a few expensive and peculiar items like a working "melted" wristwatch.

Visual Addiction

by Robert Williams

1989; 95 pp.

$23.95 ppd (CA residents add sales tax) from: Last Gasp,
2180 Bryant St., San Francisco, CA 94110; 415-824-6636

Combining imagery from carnival midway art, psychedelia, comic books, hot rods, pulp science fiction and mystery magazines, and "trash" art (softcore porn, graffiti, tattoos, etc.), Robert Williams becomes sort of a billboard painter for Bedlam, U.S.A. His work is funny and harrowing; backbrain fantasies crossed with consumer society fear and loathing. No question about it, he's my choice to do the next official presidential portrait. With an intro by Lydia Lunch.

SOURCES

Book Sources

2.13.61, P.O. Box 1910, Los Angeles, CA 90078; 213-462-8962; newsletter free

Excellent human being, Henry Rollins' publishing and distribution house. Books by Rollins, Hubert Selby, Howard Devoto, Lydia Lunch & Exene Cervenka, others. Rollins' spoken word tapes, CDs and T-shirts.

A Different Light, 548 Hudson Street, NY, NY 10014; 800-343-4002; fax 212-989-2158; catalog free

Gay and lesbian zines and books from both major and small presses. Around 10,000 titles in stock. If it's not in the catalog, ask for it.

AMOK Fourth Dispatch, 1764 N. Vermont Ave., L.A., CA 90027; catalog $14.95; for orders 800-782-6657

Why drop fifteen bucks on a book catalog? When the catalog is a mind-altering book all on its own. Intensity of interest is the key idea in AMOK-land. Where Facial Rejuvenative Surgery, the CIA entrance examination, An Album of Mayan Architecture, Girls Who Do Stag Movies, and the works of Nabokov and Flannery O'Connor can exist almost side by side, anything is possible.

Delta Manuals, P.O. Box 1751, 716 Harrell Street, El Dorado, AR 71731; 501-862-2077; catalog $2

Amazing collection of government-issue military handbooks: field manuals (chemical warfare, combat communications, etc.), technical manuals (night vision, medical, light weapons, etc.) and technical bulletins on World War II, and the Korean and Vietnam wars.

Flatland, P.O. Box 2420, Fort Bragg, CA 95437-2420; catalog $4 (includes quarterly updates)

Non-fiction books, extreme literature, zines and independent periodicals covering covert interests: UFOs, Situationist lit, conspiracy theories, AIDS, health and orgone info.

Last Gasp, 2180 Bryant St., San Francisco, CA 94110; 415-824-6636; catalog $2

One of the best book catalogs around. If you're awake, you will covet something in here: underground comics, literature, art, drugs, crime, magic, women's lit, body modification, erotica, music, weird games, odd trading cards and, yes, even cookbooks.

Manga-chan (and/or My Friend in Japan), 2-10-3-301 Minami Kugahara, Ota-ku Tokyo 146, Japan; or 1750 30th St., #312, Boulder, CO 80301, USA; or email: manga@oldcolo.com; voice/fax 81-3-5600-3614

Basically any cool thing you want from Japan: books, manga, video games, Japanimation, CDs. Email or fax for

current catalog. They can also do searches for special items. Payment by money order, bank transfer or cash.

Loompanics Unlimited, P.O. Box 1197, Port Townsend, WA 98368; catalog $5

Their catalog says it all: "(Loompanics) is an important source for anarchists, survivalists, iconoclasts, self-liberators, mercenaries... and just about anyone interested in the strange, the useful, the arcane, the oddball, the unusual, the unique and the diabolical." Titles range from obviously useful topics like self-publishing to barely legal texts on fake IDs, explosives and self-defense.

Office of Technological Assessment, U.S. Congress, Washington, D.C. 20510-8025, ATTN: Publications Requests; 202-224-8996; fax 202-228-6098

The OTA prints reports for Congress on "emerging, difficult and often highly technical issues." You can get these same reports. Topics range from drug testing to acid rain to research into brain grafting. Most reports are under $20; many are much cheaper.

Schoenhof's Foreign Books, 76A Mt. Auburn Street, Cambridge, MA; 617-547-8855; fax 617-547-8551

Dozens of European languages in their reference section, and almost as many in literature. Their reference book catalog is comprehensive, but their literature catalog only covers Spanish, German, French and Italian. Call or fax for titles in other languages.

Sexuality Library, 1210 Valencia St., San Francisco, CA 94110; catalog $2; 415-550-7399; fax 415-550-8495

Your one-stop sex info shop. Catalog features books, videos and zines on virtually any aspect of sexuality—female, male, gay, straight, children's and adolescents' sexuality, sex info for older people, erotic literature, humor, sexual politics and "sex for one."

Tattered Cover Bookstore; 800-833-9327

This bookstore has no catalog, but they have a big stock of books from around the world; if they don't have something, they'll order it, even from England. They take charge cards, but will send your order with a bill, and let you remit by check. Hours: 9:30-9 M-F, Sat 9:30-6, Sun 12-5, MST.

Mark V. Ziesing, P.O. Box 76, Shingletown, CA 96088; 916-474-1580; catalog free

Outstanding selection of science fiction, fantasy and *outré* literature. Ziesing also carries lots of small press, art books, zines and British first editions for collectors. Ziesing is also a small press publisher of high-quality hardbacks by Kim Stanley Robinson, Pat Cadigan, Lucius Shepard, Bruce Sterling and others.

zines

Introduction—Zines

It took the printed word a long time to become democratic. In the West, at least, the whole words-on-paper game was an upper class pursuit at the height of the Greek and Roman toga party days. After that, it pretty much became a monopoly of the Catholic Church, which controlled what was written and who got to see it. The guy who broke the bank, of course, was that early hardware hacker, Johann Gutenberg, who retrofit a wine press with moveable type— and all he wanted to do was scam some quick cash from the religious rabble by selling them fake indulgences. And even when the printing press became motorized and ubiquitous, the thing was still too hard to operate and too expensive for individuals to own. Early attempts at cheap text duplication weren't entirely satisfactory: mimeograph machines, for instance, stank like a toxic waste dump and turned your fingers nerve-gas blue. Even with this primitive tool, it didn't take long for people to start creating their own little magazines, or zines. These small publications were mostly labors of love, which turned little or no profit. Generally, they were a way for people with an obsession, or a determined need to tell you how they felt, to get their thoughts down on paper and out into the world.

Every month, all over the world, new little zines are mailing out their first issues, while others struggle to finish their last. Mike Gunderloy, the creator of *Factsheet Five*, and co-author of **The World of Zines** (see review, page 57), estimates that there are at least 10,000 zines being published in the United States alone. Because many zines publish irregularly on a micro-budget (and most don't take ads), the editors feel free to say whatever pops into their heads; this makes zines probably the closest thing to a direct link between the brain and the printed page.

The topics addressed in these zines are as varied as their points of view. In this one chapter's small sampling, you'll find zines dedicated to hacking computer systems, body modification, life extension, the possibilities of virtual reality sex, smart drugs, life inside the U.S. prison system, cryptozoology (the study of animals that might not exist), the intelligence community, cross-dressing, and religion. Other zines specifically dedicated to music and video are listed in those sections.

But the zine world doesn't stop with the printed page anymore. The same computer revolution that put desktop publishing at the end of everyone's mouse has allowed the zine world to invade cyberspace, and give birth to a whole new breed of zine: the electronic, or "Ezine." These are zines that exist on one or more computer bulletin board systems; many Ezines have no print version at all, existing only as cleverly arranged electrons on hard disks around the country, accessible to anyone with a computer and a modem. Andy Hawks, the editor of his own Ezine, *Future Culture*, has put together a list of some of the best online zines (pages 81 and 82).

One last note about purchasing zines: Some of the zines listed here are simple typewritten, photocopied and stapled pages; others are glossy, slick four-color productions with predictable schedules and ad rates. When you're buying copies of some of the lower-priced zines, you'll make life easier for the editors if you send cash; that way they don't have to deal with banks, currency conversion, etc. Just be sure to fold the bills inside your cover letter.

Factsheet 5

$20/2 years (6 issues; $40 Canada & Mexico; $50 overseas; $6 sample copy; CA residents add sales tax) from: Factsheet 5, c/o R. Seth Friedman, P.O. Box 170099, San Francisco, CA 94117-0099; print version email: sethf5@well.sf.ca.us; online version email: jerod23@well.sf.ca.us

Factsheet 5 is nothing less than the Rosetta Stone of the zine world. It's where you go to find out what zines are out there, what they're about and how you can get your mitts on them. Each *F5* issue brings you the lowdown on hundreds and hundreds of zines covering everything from stamp collecting to Zen Buddhism, from mail art to animal rights, from white Aryan nutcases to Green communal living. *F5* is one of the few items under the sun that truly has "something for everyone." Plus, it's indexed!

And now for those who can't wait for the mails, or who don't need more stuff cluttering up their house, *F5* is also online. And it's free! There are a number of ways to get the electronic *F5* straight into your computer. The easiest way is to subscribe via email. There are three email categories: "subscribe issue," "subscribe update" and "subscribe both." "Issue" subscribers are emailed from twenty to thirty files, the rough equivalent of an *F5* print issue, about every 4 months. "Update" subscribers receive files whenever new ones become available, anywhere from twice a week to once a month. A "both" subscription will get you files whenever they are updated, plus the regular compilation of files put together in a complete electronic *F5* issue. To subscribe to the electronic *F5*, send email to: jerod23@well.sf.ca.us; in the "subject" line of the email, just enter "subscribe issue," "subscribe update" or "subscribe both." That's it.

If you want to take a look at the electronic *F5* before subscribing, they are stored as downloadable FTP files at red.css.itd.umich.edu in /pub/Factsheet.Five. They're also available via gopher from gopher.well.sf.ca.us. There is also an ongoing *Factsheet Five* conference on the WELL teleconferencing system. The WELL costs $15 a month, plus $2 an hour. It's located in the San Francisco area, but there are lots of logon sites around the country, so you can avoid long distance charges. To register, set your modem to dial 415-332-7217; type "newuser" at the prompt, and go from there. If you want to talk to an actual person, call 415-332-4335.

The World of Zines

(A Guide to the Independent Magazine Revolution)
by Mike Gunderloy & Cari Goldberg Janice

$17 ppd (CA residents add sales tax) from: Whole Earth Review, 27
Gate Five Rd., Sausalito, CA 94965; order number 800-938-6657

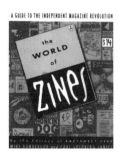

Little did Mike Gunderloy realize when he started *Factsheet Five*
years ago, that he would be aiding and abetting a whole movement
of independent writers and publishers. Gunderloy has since passed
F5 on to new, fresh hands, but not before putting what he learned
into **The World of Zines**; co-edited with Cari Goldberg Janice, the
book is a distillation of their zine experience. **The World of Zines**
contains reviews of the 400 hottest zines around, plus a history of
zine publishing and, maybe most important, a primer on how you
can start your own zine. This is an excellent place to enter the
zine world.

Zine Exchange Network

Send a zine and SASE to: Zine Exchange Network, P.O. Box 7052,
Austin, TX 78713

If you've already produced your own zine, regardless of the subject
matter, here's a quick and easy way to enter the world of zine barter-
ing. Just send a copy of your zine (along with an SASE) to the Zine
Exchange Network, and you'll get back a new zine in return. What
you receive is pretty random; it depends on who else has sent stuff
to Z.E.N., and how much return postage you've put on your return
envelope. You can request subject areas, but that's about as specific
as the Z.E.N. folks will get. Think of it as an adventure, sort of the
print equivalent of a blind date.

2600

$21/year (4 issues) from: 2600, P.O. Box 752, Middle Island, NY 11953-0752; 516-751-2600; FAX 516-751-2608; email: 2600@well.sf.ca.us

The first, and still the only indispensable document of the hacker/phreaker world. *2600* dares to publish unmentionables such as the intricate anatomy of wire and cellular phone systems, satellite access and the postal bar code system, often using documents supplied straight from the companies they're hacking.

But *2600* doesn't restrict its gaze to the digital world; the whole realm of information access is open to them, and they dearly love to expose supposedly "uncrackable" systems. One of their more interesting targets was Federal Express dropoff boxes which use the allegedly "maximum security" Simplex lock system. The *2600* testing teams were able to open these super locks in an average of ten minutes. While this might not seem important on its face, the fact is that Simplex locks are also used at some government offices because of their "unhackable" reputation.

If you're interested in worming your way into someone else's information, protecting your own, or you're looking for the edge of the information frontier, you need look no further than *2600*.

Black Ice

£23/year (4 issues; £15 U.K.; £20 Europe) from: Black Ice, Subscription Dept., P.O. Box 1069, Brighton BN2 4YT, U.K.

Not to be confused with the American literary zine of the same name, this British cyberzine has the same restless intensity and adventurous spirit of early punk bands (along with some of the same sloppiness in execution). And like punk, there's a different feel to the U.K. and U.S. versions. The design is as frenzied as *any* cyberculture rag, but some of the we're-the-cutting-edge posing of the American edition is thankfully absent here, and in its place is a genuine sense of humor. Topics in their first issue range from homebrew VR to media agitprop to Japanese junk food.

Answer Me!

$4.50/issue ($3.50 bulk mail) from: Goad To Hell Enterprises, 6520 Selma Ave., #1171, Hollywood, CA 90028

Simply put, *Answer Me!*'s proprietors, Mr. and Ms. Goad, don't care what you think, don't like you and would probably like you even less if they met you. Their zine carries on this neighborly tradition with such inspirational articles as "The Family Must Be Eliminated!," "People Ruin Everything" and the lovely duet, "I Hate Women"/"I Hate Men." Each issue is rounded out nicely by interviews with such uplifting characters as exploitation film director Ray Dennis Steckler, porn king Al Goldstein and Anton LaVey, the guy who pretty much made Satanism a paying concern in America.

In short, reading *Answer Me!* is sort of the equivalent of a cultural mugging made amusing.

Back Brain Recluse

$36/year (4 issues) from: Anne Marsden, 1052 Calle del Cerro, #708, San Clemente, CA 92672-6068

Back Brain Recluse, a British science fiction zine, publishes some of the most startling and daring science fiction currently being written, emphasizing the experimental and most uncommercial end of the form. Brits like Michael Moorcock and Diana Reed contribute alongside American authors like Misha and Paul Di Filippo. *BBR* also publishes fine, and occasionally brilliant, artwork. If you think you know what science fiction looks like, think again.

Bad Attitude

$24/year (6 issues; $40 foreign) from: Bad Attitude, P.O. Box 390110, Cambridge, MA 02139

A radical lesbian sex/smut/political zine. It's similar to the Big Sister of radical lesbian zines, *On Our Backs* (see review on page 72), in its we're-here-we're-horny-and-we-aren't-interested-in-politcally-correct-sex outlook, but *Bad Attitude* is less slick, and more down and dirty. Hot fiction, nonfiction, cartoons, letters, photos and graphics.

Black Leather Times

$8/year (4 issues; $12 foreign) from: Black Leather Times, 3 Calabar Court, Gaithersburg, MD 20877

I could have told you this would happen if you let punks get hold of computers and xerox machines—jokes about suicide, vicious and nasty "advice" columns, stories about giving poor little kids potatoes instead of candy on Halloween, and why you should ditch your family Thanksgiving dinner. Jokes about drugs! Stories about bad sex! Jokes about cannibalism! Nice graphics too. And now they've started their own erotica/fetish spin-off zine, *Blue Blood*.

Punks with computers. You've been warned.

Body Play

(& Modern Primitives Quarterly)
$45/year (4 issues; $12 sample copy) from: Insight Books, c/o Subscriptions, Box 421668, San Francisco, CA 94142-1668

Fakir Musafar, one of the stars of RE/Search's notorious **Modern Primitives** book, now has his own body modification zine. It's quite a beautiful document, on heavy paper with excellent photos, both new and archival. Topics in the first issue include What is *Body Play*? Corsets (tiny waist fetishism), branding (just like on cattle—and you thought your piercing made you butch...), tattoos as jewelry, and the yogic practice of "Uddiyana Bandha," a technique where practitioners literally pull their belly back into their bodies, causing their midsections to all but disappear. Of course, there's also a resource directory and information on related zines and books.

Small, or wasp waist, discipline from *Body Play*.

bOING-bOING

$14/year (4 issues; $3.95 sample copy) from: bOING-bOING, 11288 Ventura Blvd. #818, Studio City, CA 91602; email: mark@well.sf.ca.us

LA-based cyberzine that both extols the virtues of and laughs at neo-tech culture. Literate and attractive without showing off, it's one of the few cyberculture publications where words still matter. Recent issues have featured interviews with authors Lewis Shiner and Bruce Sterling, a report on the third-annual Artificial Life conference, smart drug reports, reviews of way cool software, DIY CDs and robot groupies. Plus book, zine and music reviews. Essential reading for the culturally online.

Covert Action Quarterly

$19/year (4 issues) from: Covert Action Publications, 1500 Massachusetts Ave. NW, Washington, D.C. 20005; 202-331-9763

An intelligence community watchdog magazine put together by actual ex-spooks. They used to blow the cover of various U.S. spies, but that's illegal these days. Now they mostly do a lot of investigative work, reporting on covert operations overseas and disinformation campaigns at home. This isn't dry, impartial journalism. These guys are pissed off...You won't read any of these stories in the mainstream press (at least, not until all the action is over).

CrimeBeat Magazine

$19.95/year (12 issues; $27.95 Canada) from: CrimeBeat Magazine, P.O. Box 438, Mt. Morris, IL 61054; 800-877-5303

New street crimes, cops gone renegade, three-card monte scams and guns, guns, guns, they're all in *CrimeBeat*, "The Monthly Newsmagazine of Crime." This is actually pretty entertaining, hitting both the high and low points of crime infotainment. In one issue, you're likely to get features on new gun laws, sexual harassment and the future of capital punishment, interspersed with tidbits like big city crime tours and the best true-crime films. Don't blame me, though, if by the end of an issue you're turning on all the lights and checking all the locks. Even the ads are paranoia-inducing.

Cross-Talk

$36/year (12 issues; $5 sample copy; $7 foreign; make checks payable to Kymberleigh Richards) from: Cross-Talk, P.O. Box 944, Woodland Hills, CA 91365

A newszine for the transvestite and transsexual community. *Cross-Talk* recently upgraded from its newsletter format, and the change is welcome, both in design and readability. Cross-dressing hints from experts. Fiction and some very funny cartoons. True-life tales of "passing." Lists of national hotlines and events. Lots of ads for shops that carry bigger sizes of female clothes to fit guys.

Cryonics

$35/year (12 issues; $40 Canada and Mexico; $45 overseas) from: ALCOR, 12327 Doherty St., Riverside, CA 93503; 800-367-2228; email: alcor@cup.portal.com

For anyone contemplating being frozen on or near death, this is your zine. Part information source, part ad tool and part propaganda, *Cryonics* not only lucidly and seriously discusses the culture of life extension, it attempts to bring some credibility to a system that's just barely legal in this country. Articles on how to prepare your finances before you're frozen. Blow-by-blow descriptions of the freezing process. Fighting bureaucrats for the acceptance of freezing as a legitimate medical tool. Cryonics and libertarianism. Copious photos of the freezing process and storage facilities.

Diseased Pariah News

$7/year (4 issues; $10 Canada; $18 Overseas) from: DPN, P.O. Box 31431, San Francisco, CA 94131; 510-891-0455

"The *Diseased Pariah News* is a quarterly publication of, by, and for people with HIV disease. We are a forum for infected people to share their thoughts, feelings, art, writing, and brownie recipes in an atmosphere free of teddy bears, magic rocks and seronegative guilt." This is also one of the most beautifully produced independent zines around. *DPN* dishes up copious amounts of black humor, safe sex info, and very personal features on, for instance, "How I Got AIDS" and what it's like getting busted at ACT-UP rallies. Whether you're gay, straight or bi, this is a zine you shouldn't miss.

Extropy

$30/year (6 issues) from: Extropy, P.O. Box 77243, Los Angeles, CA 90007-0243; email: more@usc.edu

"The Journal of Transhumanist Thought," explains the subtitle. While physically small, this is a serious-minded zine, dense with ideas and data, put together by a group trying to lay the foundation for rational thought and action in the technologically-exploding world of the near future. Their areas of interests/obsessions include life extension, Artificial Intelligence, smart drugs, space habitation, artificial life, nanotechnology and "futurist morality." Imagine a zine written by the characters in a Bruce Sterling story.

Forced Exposure

$13/year (4 issues) from: Forced Exposure, P.O. Box 9102, Waltham, MA 02254

Excellent blend of rock & roll, art and reviews. What separates *Forced Exposure* from other "alternative" music and art magazines is the intelligence and intensity of its editorial style. One recent issue contained a profile of guitar experimenter/improviser Henry Kaiser, an excerpt from Sonic Youth's tour diary, an interview with Beat-influenced postmodern painter Robert Williams, plus reviews of Black Lizard Press' line of revived pulp thrillers. *Forced Exposure* is *Rolling Stone* for people who'd rather read the *Journal of Trauma Medicine* than watch MTV.

Author and hacker, Rudy Rucker discusses chaos theory and surfing in *Forced Exposure.*

Frighten the Horses

$16/year (4 issues; $5 sample issue) from: Heat Seeking Publishing, 41 Sutter Street, #1108, San Francisco, CA 94104

Mark Pritchard's excellent quarterly is subtitled "a document of the sexual revolution," and it easily lives up to that claim, combining equal doses of intelligence and heat. *FTH* features well-written fiction and nonfiction (often addressing issues of censorship and activism) for men and women of all sexual preferences, by authors such as Rachel Kaplan, Carol Queen, Pat Califia, Andy Dunn and Pritchard himself. This is also one of the few magazines that publishes erotic poetry that isn't so sweet and pure and politically correct that you want to puke.

Future Sex

$18/year (4 issues; CA residents add sales tax) from: Future Sex, 1095 Market St., #809, San Francisco, CA 94103-9670

Where lust and the digital world meet, *Future Sex* is there. Lots of sex software discussions and reviews, from currently available games, to modem-accessible bulletin boards full of digitized naked people, to X-rated porn loops for your computer. Virtual sex and the smart drug/lust matrix are covered. *Future Sex* strikes a nice balance between awe at the possibilities of tech sex and skepticism with the actual implementation of the hard/software. Editor Lisa Palac is smart and quick and determined to keep pushing limits; keep an eye on her zine.

Girljock

$12/year (4 issues) from: ROX-A-TRONIC, 2060 Third St., Berkeley, CA 94710

First propelling itself into the zine scene a couple of years ago, *Girljock*, "the magazine for the athletic lesbian, but not entirely about sports," has gone through a startling adolescence, sprouting from a hand-scrawled digest-sized zine to a full-bodied 8-1/2" x 11" format with readable type and half-toned photos. *Girljock* remains, however, the same irreverent collection of stories, cartoons, confessionals, interviews and tales of nude surfing as when editor Roxxie first said, "Fuck the Well of Loneliness. Goodbye to all that. We're here to have fun."

Gnosis

$18/year (6 issues; $25 foreign; CA residents add sales tax) from: Gnosis Magazine, P.O. Box 14217, San Francisco, CA 94114

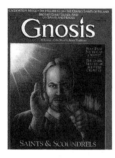

Gnosis is "dedicated to the dissemination of information about the esoteric spritual traditions of the West." But it's not nearly as stern as it might first sound. *Gnosis* is a seriously minded, though quite undour, look at spiritual systems by a group of writers and artists, many of whom are quite active in underground and fringe publishing: Jay Kinney, R.A. Wilson, Ted Schulz, etc.

Each issue of *Gnosis* revolves around a core theme, such as Saints & Scoundrels, Groups & Communities, Alchemy, The Goddess, The Trickster and Holy War. The writing and graphics are lively and sometimes funny, while always respectful of different belief systems. *Gnosis* gives you a chance to see the way disparate groups define themselves and the world they live in.

Gray Areas

$18/year (4 issues; $26 foreign; PA residents add sales tax) from: Gray Areas, P.O. Box 808, Broomall, PA 19008-0808

Although they're identified broadly as a Grateful Dead zine, *Gray Areas* is much more than that. Along with the mandatory music and video reviews, they track culture on the edge of change, things like copyright issues (the Grateful Dead allows people to freely bootleg their shows and, in an interview, Frank Zappa tells how he bootlegs his bootlegs), computer crime (in an interview with John Barlow of the Electronic Frontier Foundation), new female-run adult movie businesses, and drug testing. A smart and attractive zine that is definitely not just for Deadheads.

Holy Titclamps

$5/year (3 issues; $2 sample copy) from: Larry-bob, P.O. Box 591275, San Francisco, CA 94159-1275

Loud, funny and not-in-any-way shy queerzine. Fiction, cartoons, lots of naked and semi-naked guys and a few dykes. Reports from Radical Faeries, drag queens, poetry, letters and reports and slams from the zine world. Also, each issue of *Holy Titclamps* includes editor Larry-bob's extensive queerzine review/contact info. You can get the zine list in a separate booklet for just two first-class stamps; the list is also available as a Hypercard stack for $2. You can order both from the address above.

Intertek

$4/issue, or $14/4 issues (2 years; overseas $5.25/issue & $18.25/4 issues) from: Intertek, c/o Steve Steinberg, 13 Daffodil Lane, San Carlos, CA 94070

Smart, informative and serious (as opposed to flashy) cyberzine by an editor who knows what's going on. A recent issue covers Virtual Communities, groups of people scattered all over the world who are nonetheless intimately linked by computer bulletin boards and conferencing systems. Previous issues have covered designer drugs, the world of hacking, and ethics in cyberculture.

Interzone

$52/year (12 issues) from: Interzone, 217 Preston Drove, Brighton BN1 6FL, United Kingdom

Interzone pretty much revived the moribund British SF short fiction world in the early 80s. Unlike its cousin, *Back Brain Recluse*, *Interzone*'s fictions are more traditionally literary in style, which is not to say stuffy, merely that they are well-written and intelligent tales with beginnings, middles and ends. Not as wild as *BBR*, but not as inconsistent either. Some of the best Brit and U.S. writers have graced its pages, including William Gibson, J.G. Ballard, Karen Joy Fowler, Geoff Ryman, Richard Calder, Lisa Tuttle, and on and on. *BBR* and *Interzone* are great complements to each other.

It's a Wonderful Lifestyle

$4/issue from: Candi Strecker, 590 Lisbon, San Francisco, CA 94112

This is Candi Strecker's (of *Sidney Suppey's Quarterly & Confused Pet Monthly* fame; see review on page 75) anthropological trilogy of 70s culture. In just the first issue you get Disco, scary clothes, scarier shoes, cool 70s cars, Mary Hartman, and a discussion of the film that became the moral barometer of a generation, managing to be both pacifist and fascist at the same time—*Billy Jack*!

Parts two and three are in the works.

Jack Ruby Slippers

$2/issue from: Jack Ruby Slippers, 1800 Market Street, # 258, San Francisco, CA 94102

Visual assault, information assault, assumption assault. Crypto-Situationist, cyber-something, Burroughsian dispatches from the dystopian heart of a corporate xerox machine (on the sly, of course). The Information War is here. Why fight it? Like Lux Interior says, "Blow up your mind!"

TOTAL WAR HAS BECOME INFORMATION WAR

IT IS BEING FOUGHT NOW

Komotion International

$10/year (includes Komotion International membership) from: Komotion International, P.O. Box 410502, San Francisco, CA 94141-0502

A San Francisco-area artists' collective that publishes its own print zine, sponsors performance events and creates its own music cassettes and videos. Membership includes the zine, plus performance listings and discounts to shows. The print zine is a forum for political discussions of all sorts (Gulf War resistance, the clash of culture and commerce, the role of disinformation in the media), as well as a haven for fiction, poetry and memorable graphics.

Living Free

$9/year (6 issues; $12 foreign; make checks payable to Jim Stumm) from: Jim Stumm, Living Free, P.O. Box 29, Hiler Branch, Buffalo, NY 14223

Does virtually everything about society (especially urban society) bug you? Then *Living Free* might be your meat. This libertarian, DIY zine is devoted to letting you know that you can take care of yourself, without government (or most anyone else's) help. It's a back-to-the-land philosophy that isn't about tree-hugging, but about creating a sustainable and hassle-free life for yourself. Reviews of helpful books on, for instance, hydroponic gardening, useful zines and discussions of alternate forms of government round out each issue. *Living Free* isn't the prettiest zine around, but it packs a wealth of information into just a few pages.

Logomotive

$18/year (4 issues; $5 sample issue; include signed statement of age) from: Logomotive, P.O. Box 3101, Berkeley, CA 94703

Logomotive calls itself the "little sex zine that does," and with their second issue it does indeed. This is one of a new breed of sex zines that calls itself "queer," as opposed to gay or bi or straight or bent at 36 degrees. The term "queer" in this context means that *Logomotive's* sexuality and eroticism is all over the map, appealing to almost anyone who is curious and open. *Logomotive's* non-fiction is smart, and its fiction ranges from hot to hilarious, and is sometimes both. Great graphics, too.

Magazine of the Month Club

$39.25/year (12 issues; $9.95, 3 issues; $19.75, 6 issues) from: Multinewspapers, P.O. Box 866, Dana Point, CA 92629

Imagine getting a different English-language magazine every month, and each issue is from somewhere else in the world. Multinewspapers, a distributor of periodicals from all over the world, has loads of English-language zines from places like England, Greece, Spain, Zimbabwe, France and Australia. Join their club and you might get a gardening zine from Ireland or a UFO zine from

England. If you're really greedy (or just adventurous) you can get two zines a month with a Magazine of the Month Club "double subscription," which brings you a new zine every two weeks (the price of the double subs are roughly twice those of the prices listed above).

Well punk, do you feel lucky...?

Monk

$18/year (8 issues) from: Monk, 175 Fifth Ave., Suite 2322, NY, NY 10010; 212/465-3231

Take two slightly off-center guys, add one motorhome and a Macintosh, and you get *Monk*, the first postmodern travel magazine.

Monk is travel writing made absurd—stories about people the guys meet in diners, their marriages and breakups, nut cases in New York trying to break into their camper, the cat they adopted at a rest stop, and tall tales from the road ("Drag Queens Invade Midwestern High School!"). There are even a few celebrity interviews thrown in—such as goddess/slut Annie Sprinkle—whenever the *Monk* guys happen to run into a celebrity. *Monk* is travel writing made twistedly and uniquely personal. Imagine the David Lynch version of Travels With Charley.

Murder Can Be Fun

Issues 1-4 $.60 each; 5-8 $.70 each; 9-13 $1.25 each; (Anti) Sex Tips for Teens $1.25 from: John Marr, Box 640111, San Francisco, CA 94109

If Hannibal "The Cannibal" Lecter ran a fanzine out of his asylum cell, it would probably look a lot like *Murder Can Be Fun*. They're all here—your favorite mass murderers, serial killers and natural disasters documented with painstaking care. If this sounds like bad taste, it is, but it's bad taste with a lot of humor and intellectual rigor.

Editor John Marr has also spun-off his taste for the absurd into (Anti) Sex Tips for Teens: The Teen Advice Book 1897-1987, a collection of frighteningly moronic etiquette and advice tidbits from Pat Boone and other social scholars.

Mondo 2000

$21/year (5 issues) from: Mondo 2000, P.O. Box 10171, Berkeley, CA 94709; email: mondo2000@mcimail.mci.com

The most self-conscious fashion-statement cyberzine around is constantly betrayed by its form; it's a post-literate artifact, yet it's burdened with words. No matter, really. The graphics are spectacular, so you don't really have to read anything. In fact, reading *Mondo 2000* is becoming harder and harder. In recent issues the zine's contents have achieved a kind of frictionless sheen, so that your eye slips effortlessly from article to ad to article to fashion layout to artist profile, and on and on. Of course this is all intentional, which is what makes it fascinating. *Mondo 2000* itself is a vision of the future, a neon bright bauble, part snake oil and part revelation. And no matter how hard the editors try, they can't help but let a little useful information leak into each issue.

News of the Weird

$7/year (7 issues; $11 for both News of the Weird and View from the Ledge; make checks payable to Chuck Shepherd) from: Chuck Shepherd, P.O. Box 8306, St. Petersburg, FL 33738

News of the Weird contains clippings of the weirdest, dumbest, most awful or most peculiar stories pulled from newspapers all over the country. Four solidly-packed pages every seven weeks.

Editor Chuck Shepherd also produces a companion zine, *View from the Ledge*. Similar to *News of the Weird*, but with little overlap of material, and *View from the Ledge* also contains actual ads that are either too insane or too stupid to be described and must be seen (such as the "cute mom and child giggling" funeral home ad). My recommendation is that you subscribe to both. Together, they're one of the few true bargains left.

- *Gary Blantz, 29, was arrested for kidnapping a bar owner near Lancaster, PA, in February. Police reported later that Blantz shot himself in the foot with his .45 caliber revolver to show the victim what would happen to him if he were disobedient.*

Nootropic News

$12/year (4 issues) from: Nootropic News, P.O. Box 177, Camarillo, CA 93011

Nootropic News is right in the thick of the smart drug scene, and isn't afraid to tell you to take these drugs now if you want to grease those synapses for heavy computing in the world to come. Reviews of medical literature on smart drugs. Synergistic effects of nootropics. Legal advice and the smart drug scene. Memory-enhancement effects of vasopressin. Reports on FDA clamp-downs on drug importers.

With an SASE, you can also get data sheets with recommended dosages of smart drugs, lists of suppliers and FDA "import alerts." *Nootropic News* also sells some of its own info books. This zine is a nice companion to *Smart Drug News* (see review on page 76).

The Nose

$15/year (6 issues) from: The Nose, 1095 Market Street, # 812, San Francisco, CA 94103

Open up the skull of *Spy* magazine and reveal the brain. Using your scalpel, excise major portions of the "Smugness" and "Snide" centers, while grafting new "Humor" tissue into place. Liberally soak the entire brain pan in the IQ-boosting smart drug of your choice, and close. Attach electrodes and jolt the beast. When it begins to mumble about three-picture deals or says, "You call yourself a mad scientist? I've seen scarier stock-boys at Wal-Mart," your job is done. Call the beast *The Nose*, a California-based humor magazine dissecting the West. Buy. Subscribe. You have no choice.

Poppin' Zits!

$3/issue from: Jerod Pore, 1800 Market St., #141, San Francisco, CA 94102-6227

Collage zine. Weird pix. Stolen data. Information overload. Porn and science. Microbes and S&M. Robots and dames. Strange manifestos. Naked firemen. If William Burroughs' head exploded, *Poppin' Zits!* is what you might find on the walls.

On Our Backs

$34.95/year (6 issues) from: On Our Backs, 526 Castro Street, San Francisco, CA 94114

Subtitled "Entertainment for the Adventurous Lesbian," it's a direct reply to many dour anti-sex "womyn's" magazines. The editors are relentless in their pursuit of the politically incorrect; ex-editor Susie Bright even used one of her columns to recount having and enjoying sex with a man in order to get pregnant. *On Our Backs* features excellent fiction, non-fiction and art guaranteed to delight/piss off just about everyone.

Pills-a-go-go

$12/year (6 issues; $2 sample issue) from: Pills-a-go-go, 1202 E. Pike St., # 849, Seattle, WA 98122-3934

Pills. Good pills, bad pills. Pills that jack you up, and pills that melt your bones. Celebrity pills. Banned pills and about-to-be-banned pills. Smart pills. Poison pills. Lawsuits over pills. The FDA and pills. Computers and pills. No judgments, just info. And pills.

• *Thanks to the* New York Times *paying a janitor $200 to steal documents from the prosecutor's desk (the* NYT *denies this) we now know that (Jeffery) Dahmer used Halcion to knock out a 13-year-old boy in 1988. Traces of unspecified benzodiazapines were found in two of the corpses recovered from the notorious apartment along with an unfilled prescription for lorazapam (another benzodiazapine). Halcion and alcohol seem like a great combo for rendering someone unconscious. Not lorazapam.*

P.O.N.Y. X-Press

$20/year (4 issues; $6.50 sample issue) from: PONY X-Press, 25 West 45th Street, #1401, New York, NY 10036

A zine by and for the New York City sex workers' community. A report on condom art installation in the window of the New Museum of Contemporary Art. Annie Sprinkle's favorite trick. Health tips for sex workers. A prostitute's "Letter from London." Sex industry-positive articles such as, "Prostitution is My Sexual Preference." News snippets from around the world. Lists of sex workers organizations and events, ads and classifieds.

Presence

$50/year (4 issues;) from: MIT Press Journals, 55 Hayward St., Cambridge, MA 02142-9902

MIT has always been a leader in tech-oriented theory zines. *Presence* is their newest venture, a showcase for developments in the rapidly expanding world of virtual reality. Unlike pop cyberzines such as *bOING-bOING*, *Mondo 2000* and *Wired*, *Presence* is about as user-friendly as a cruise missile. Theory abounds, but so do heavy equations and pages of mathematical tables. Still, if you want to see how a new technology is being invented as it's happening, this is the place to do it.

Recent articles include a look at new position trackers, tactile feedback in teleoperations, artists' experiments with VR and virtual sound research. Info on upcoming VR events, reviews and interesting ads.

Prison Life

$19.95/year (6 issues; $3.95 sample copy; $60 foreign) from: Prison Life Subscription Dept., 111 S. Ninth Street, Suite 3, Columbia, MO 65201

Talk about a special interest zine—this one is strictly about life in and around the U.S. prison system. Many of the articles concern specific prisoners, some of whom—like Wilbert Rideau, editor of the inmate-operated *The Angolite* magazine—have turned their lives around while doing time. Other articles focus on prisoners who seem lost in some Kafkaesque dream, like the inmate convicted of murder who has offered to sell off some of his organs to raise money for an appeal. Still other stories focus on the parts of the prison system that seem to work (like the PATCH program that allows female prisoners to spend time with their children in a home-like environment) to the parts that don't (like the current parole system, where high-profile prisoners are singled out for special, sometimes abusive, treatment). *Prison Life* is a weird cross between titillation and information, a four-color dispatch from a gray, grim world.

Quarterly Review of Doublespeak

$8/year (4 issues) from: National Council of Teachers of English, 1111 Kenyon Rd., Urbana, IL 61801

What is doublespeak? According to the *Quarterly Review of Doublespeak* it's "inflated, overly complex, and often deliberately ambiguous language." This zine pulls together examples of double-speak from all over our society—education doublespeak, business doublespeak, military doublespeak, government and political dou-blespeak, medical doublespeak, legal doublespeak and, of course, media doublespeak. Some of the examples are hilarious, some har-rowing. Criticisms and analysis of this type of speech. Book reviews, cartoons and an extensive bibliography.

• *According to NASA, the Hubble Space Telescope has gone into "a safe mode," which means it's not working.*

Reign of Toads

$12/year (4 issues; $4 sample copy; make check payable to Kyle Silfer) from: Reign of Toads, P.O. Box 66047, Albany, NY 12206

A music-oriented zine with a lot more smarts that three-quarters of the literary-artsy-I-dance-to-the-birth-of-a-new-age rags out there. Besides lengthy overviews and interviews with bands like Ween, Robyn Hitchcock and Triptic of a Pastel Fern, they have lengthy talks with dangerous comic creators such as John Bergin, J. O'Barr and Chester Brown, chats with *Slacker* director Richard Linklater and reports on experimental instrument makers as well as the Rodney King beating. Eye-catching graphics and cartoons, plus smart book and comic reviews. This is the kind of zine that doesn't generate huge amounts of noise, but is what you really want a zine to be: smart, personal and memorable.

Science Fiction Eye

$10/year (3 issues; $15 overseas) from: Science Fiction Eye, Box 18539, Asheville, NC 28824

The only critical science fiction zine that matters, because it is the only one that traffics so smoothly in both high and low culture beyond SF. *Science Fiction Eye* casts its gaze not only on SF and SF-

related texts, but also on such topics as the work of radical artists like Stelarc and Mark Pauline, on the possibilities of consciousness-expanding chemicals and technologies, the death of Salvador Dali, and what it's like to get a movie off the ground in post-Soviet Russia. A great design, plus interviews with writers like Lucius Shepard, J.G. Ballard, and Pat Murphy, contributions from Bruce Sterling, John Shirley, Kim Stanley Robinson and Elizabeth Hand and thoughtful and occasionally savage reviews make *Science Fiction Eye* the official thought-drug of the 90s.

Sidney Suppey's Quarterly & Confused Pet Monthly

$2/issue from: Sidney Suppey Foundation, c/o Candi Strecker, 590 Lisbon, San Francisco, CA 94112

A funny and personal collection of writings, ruminations, theories, clippings, stolen and original art and more, usually on a single topic. Even when she's telling you how something really stinks, editor Candi Strecker's point of view is more ironic than furious.

Of special interest is the August 1991 issue where the editors give their less-than-reverent report on San Francisco's first (and so far, only) public virtual reality-fest, Cyberthon.

Matt Householder's Favorite example of Virtual Reality: "It's not really a horse; you don't really go anywhere, and you have to pay money to do it." From *Sidney Suppey's Quarterly*.

ZINES

Skeptical Inquirer

$25/year (4 issues) from: Skeptical Inquirer, P.O. Box 703, Buffalo, NY 14226-0703

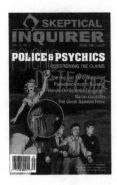

The official publication and mouthing-off journal for CSICOP, the Committee for the Scientific Investigation of Claims of the Paranormal; CSICOP's impressive membership roster boasts writers and scientists like Martin Gardner, Stephen Jay Gould and Douglas Hofstadter. *Skeptical Inquirer* is primarily a debunking zine, in which CSICOP members merrily tear into alleged UFO sightings, hauntings, psychic healings, mind-reading whizzes, "creation science" and all other manners of fringe beliefs. There is a tone of crankiness that sometimes stinks up some articles, a verbal rolling of the eyes by an author when the questions of the possible existence of poltergeists or ESP come up. But *Skeptical Inquirer*'s writers can be forgiven these occasional lapses; in an age where evangelists regularly perform miracle cures on TV, Bigfoot is still a major presence in tabloid journalism and every third person on a talk show claims to be a UFO abductee, it must be a lonely job to be the spoilsport who says, "Now wait a minute...."

Smart Drug News

$40/year (10 issues; $49 foreign) from: CERI, P.O. Box 4029, Menlo Park, CA 94026

News and tidbits from the Cognitive Enhancement Research Institute. Smart drugs in the mainstream press. Circadian rhythms and smart drug enhancement. Updates on new drugs in the pipeline. Pissed-off reviews of recent FDA decisions. How to obtain prescription drugs without a prescription. Questions and answers about specific drugs and their effects. *Smart Drug News* isn't glitzy, flashy or cute, but if you want information to know what's going on with research and legislation, this is the place to come. A nice companion to *Nootropic News* (see review on page 71).

• *L-Deprenyl is chemically related to phenethylamine (PEA), a substance found in chocolate and produced in higher-than-normal amounts in the brains of people who are "in love." L-Deprenyl's chemical structure is also closely related to amphemtaine...which causes mental stimulation.*

Strange Magazine

$17.95/2 years (4 issues; $22.95 foreign) from: Strange Magazine, P.O. Box 2246, Rockville, MD 29847

An attractive Fortean zine dedicated to cataloging and investigating all types of unexplained phenomena, including UFOs, crop circles, "falling things" (including ice, straw, sand and a human thumb), ancient astronauts and ghosts. *Strange Magazine* is also particularly big on "cryptozoology," the study of animals unknown to science, critters like the Wicomico River "Cat Man," various yeti-wannabes and modern day pterodactyls. All that plus good graphics, reviews, cartoons, and great ads.

Taste of Latex

$20/year (4 issues; $25 Canada; $40 overseas) from: Taste of Latex, P.O. Box 460122, San Francisco, CA 94146-0122

Taste of Latex is the mutant offspring of Bay Area editor/smut maven, Lily Burana. Sprung from the same restless post-punk energy that's inspired a thousand lesser zines, *TOL* is dedicated to gender-bending, -slicing and -dicing, and just plain gender-fucking. The graphics range from Michael Rosen's stunning "Sexual Portrait" photography, to politically incorrect drawings, to reader-provided shots of stunning drag queens. A recent issue features Danielle Willis' tale of boredom and banality on the set of an amateur porn movie, an interview with pioneering gay playwright Robert Chesley, a handy how-to guide to vaginal fisting, and hot fiction from Maria Jimenez. *Taste of Latex* is erotica with a rock and roll attitude.

Twilight of the Idols

$10/year (3 issues) from: John Marmysz, 3739 Balboa St., #142, San Francisco, CA 94121

Chaos-laden literary provocations. Temp-work fables and recipes for explosives. Weird poems and essays on nihilism. Cartoons and personal observations like "Notes on Pornography in Venezuela." Drinking in San Francisco and a tale from Bob Black. Barely repressed violence and high IQs. For those who prefer their coffee strong and hot, and with a slightly bitter aftertaste.

True News

$2.50/issue from: True News, 45 West 25th Street, New York, NY 10010

You know those fillers they stick in daily newspapers to make the columns come out straight? Those little paragraphs about a killer bee attack in Mexico, or about a woman who wanted to be buried with a working phone, or how some bank robber dropped his wallet on the way out of a holdup...? Now imagine if the whole paper was made up of those stories. That's pretty much what *True News* is all about. Unlike other tabloids with "I Had Bigfoot's Baby" and "The President Drives A UFO" stories splashed across the cover, all the stories in *True News* are for real, but they're just too weird, trivial, or gross to make it into the regular papers. *True News* is either the cure for, or the worst symptom yet of cultural information overload.

Unshaved Truths

$20/year (4 issues) from: Unshaved Truths, 2507 Roehampton Drive, Austin, TX 78745-6964; email: fringeware@wixer.cactus.org

Editor Jon Lebkowsky's journal of life in the cyberage features lots of twisted fiction (including the ongoing "Diary of a Programmer"), peeks inside the world of raves, the words of anarchist prostitutes, plus a mixture of poetry, commentary and reviews. In issue #3, the center spread is a two-page mini-FringeWare catalog, featuring lots of goodies for people who "hang out on the Fringes of art, society and technology." The catalog lists software, comics, funny hats, sterling silver cigarette holders, Mattel PowerGloves (which can combined with the Gold Brick Nugget board to replace the mouse attached to your Macintosh) and electronic music.

Whole Earth Review

$20/year (4 issues; $28 Canada; $26 other) from: Whole Earth Review, P.O. Box 38, Sausalito, CA 94966-9932; 800-938-6657

A quarterly extension of the **Whole Earth Catalogs** Stewart Brand produced from the late 60s through the mid-70s. *Whole Earth Review* has the same eclectic feel as those early catalogs, if not quite the bite. Still, from its original inception as the *CoEvolution*

Quarterly, until its rebirth as the *Whole Earth Review*, this zine has been at the leading edge of a lot of issues—smart drugs, bioregionalism, home computing, non-toxic living, nanotechnology—and, of course, the whole DIY-self-sufficiency ideal that sprang up in the 60s. Recent issues have tackled topics such as artificial life, ecological restoration, sex during pregnancy, electronic (computer-accessible) democracy, the status of women in the Middle East and the destruction of indigenous cultures.

Wired

$19.95/year (6 issues; $45 overseas) from: Wired, P.O. Box 191826, San Francisco, CA 94119-1826

If you spliced the thought-meme behind *Mondo 2000*, *Time* and the *Whole Earth Review*, the result would probably be something like *Wired*. In fact, one of its editors described *Wired* to me as "*Mondo 2000* for grown ups," which may be a self-contradictory phrase, but only time will tell. In truth, *Wired* has just learned to get up on its feet and toddle around the room, and like every precocious kid, it often gets into more than it can handle. The highlight of its premiere issue is Bruce Sterling's report on military virtual reality conventions. The rest of the zine strains to look dangerous and edgy but, at this stage, its butt cheeks are clenched a bit too tightly for anyone's comfort. *Wired* has great potential given its budget and the talent it can call on to fill its pages; it just has to get past the puberty blues stage and develop its own identity. If it does, stand back, because this puppy could burn brightly.

One of India's new satellite TV entrepreneurs—the "dish-wallahs." *Wallah* is a Hindi word meaning something between "hack" and "specialist."

Women & Guns

$25/year (12 issues) from: Second Amendment Foundation, Box 488, Station C, Buffalo, NY 14209; 716-885-6408

No, it's not the official Sarah Connor fan club zine, but a straight-forward firearms info publication edited by and for women. While *Women & Guns* resembles many other gun zines on the surface, the emphasis here is on self-protection, not sports. Topics addressed are basic firearms lore, learning how to choose a weapon, grips and stances, legal questions and safety. The refreshingly un-macho approach to gun information makes this a useful zine not just for women, but also men who are interested in firearms who don't want lots of articles arguing about the "killing power" of pistols the size of small dogs.

Ylem

$30/year (12 issues; $35 Canada & Mexico; $45 overseas) from: Ylem, P.O. Box 749, Orinda, CA 94563

A monthly newsletter for and about artists using technology in their work. Short articles, lists of events and exhibitions, reports from technical conferences. *Ylem* isn't a glossy four-color glitz zine for mass consumption; it's a networking tool for technically oriented artists, or those interested in their work. They also publish an annu-al directory of their nearly 300 members, with contact information; $6 for members, $15 for non-members.

Zyzzyva

$20/year (4 issues) from: Zyzzyva, 41 Sutter St., #1400, San Francisco, CA 94104-9955

A classy west coast literary zine that proves quite handily that art is alive and well outside of its east coast headquarters. Each issue of *Zyzzyva* features fine fiction, poetry, plays and graphics by known and new artists of all types. This is what literary zines used to be like—simple and straightforward in presentation, with real regard for the word and no fear of the imagination. Don't look for slice-of-life *New Yorker* minimalism here. These are works by artists who take chances.

Electronic Zines and Digests

by Andy Hawks

An electronic zine, or "Ezine" is a zine that exists only online, on a computer or a computer conferencing system; most Ezines don't have print versions. If you have a computer with a modem and are on a computer conferencing system with access to the Internet—the online connection between different conferencing systems—then you can download or subscribe to the following Ezines. Even if your system isn't on the Internet, there may be Ezines available locally. Look around the system, and don't be afraid to ask questions. —RK

Activist Times Incorporated (Internet)

Politics; hacking; anarchy. Highly recommended.

email: gzero@tronsbox.xei.com

Arm The Spirit On-Line (Autonome Forum)

Anti-capitalist/anti-imperialist Ezine.

email: aforum@moose.uvm.edu

Computers and Academic Freedom (Internet)

Computing freedom, mostly deals with college campuses.

email: listserv@eff.org <add comp-academic-freedom-news>

Computer Down-Underground Digest

Computer underground digest for Australia and New Zealand.

email: digest@hacjack.gen.nz

Computer Underground Digest (Internet)

This is required reading; it's the USA Today for the computer underground.

email: tk0jut2@niu.bitnet

Cult of the Dead Cow files

Hacking; phone phreaking; anarchy. No longer active, but downloadable FTP files are available.

FTP Files: ftp.eff.org /pub/cud/cdc

Digital Free Press (Internet)

Hacking; information.

email: dfp-req%underg@uunet.uu.net

EFF News (EFFector Online) (Internet)

EFFector Online, the Electronic Frontier Foundation's Ezine. Required reading.

email: effnews-request@eff.org

Phreaker's Bureau Int'l (Internet)

Anarchy; hacking; cyberpunk.

email: au530@cleveland.freenet.edu

High Weirdness by Email

Best of best lists; religion; science; drugs; cyberpunk; "tasteless & disgusting things;" role-playing games; rave info.

email: mporter@nyx.cs.du.edu

Informatik (Internet)

Hacking; phreaking; computer underground; cyberpunk; etc. Highly recommended.

email: inform@doc.cc.utexas.edu

Legion of Doom/Hackers Technical Journals

Hacking, brought to you by the famous masters. No longer active; FTP files available; Required reading.

FTP Files: ftp.eff.org /pub/cud/lod

Leri-L (Mailing list)

Mailing list devoted to metaprogramming, philosophy, tripping, etc.

email: leri-l@iscsvax.uni.edu

Network Information Access (Internet)

Hacking; computer underground; etc. Run by Judge Dredd. Highly recommended.

email: nia@nuchat.sccsi.com

Phrack (Internet)

Need we say more? The one, the only required hacking Ezine...

email: phrack@stormking.com

RISKS Digest (Internet)

In my humble opinion, a great must-read digest that covers all aspects of the RISKS of computing in our lives.

email: risks-request@csl.sri.com

Telecom Digest (Internet)

Infamous internet digest (also comp.dcom.telecom in Usenet) that deals with all aspects of telecommunications. Highly recommended.

email: telecom-request@eecs.nwu.edu

Telecom Privacy Digest (Internet)

Deals with privacy aspects of telecommunications (duh). Most of the conversation revolves around Caller-ID and such.

email: telecom-priv-request@pica.army.mil

Virus-l Digest (Internet)

Discussion (also virus-l on BITNET) of viruses and all aspects of 'em.

email: krvw@cert.sei.cmu.edu

Worldview - Der Weltanschaung (Internet)

Hacking; computer underground; Church of Subgenius; politics; etc. Highly recommended.

email: fox@nuchat.sccsi.com

music

Introduction—Music

On my desk, as I write this, are several precarious piles of CDs and cassettes waiting to be reviewed—pop from Morocco, Mali and Okinawa, traditional Islamic praise-singing, ambient/noise recordings from L.A. and Australia, retro-punk compilations and a whole pile of CDs from independent bands that I've never heard of. Two great forces have come together to make my desk into a Navy SEALs obstacle course and to permanently alter the face of music: jets and cheap recording equipment.

The ease of world travel and the availability of small multi-track recorders that are essentially self-contained micro-studios, means that virtually anyone can record an album and get it to anyone else on the planet. If you know where to look, most major cities now sport a variety of world and independent recordings—cassettes from Nigeria, CDs from Belgium and LPs from Jamaica, and usually a load of recordings from local bands. In the West, musicians have discovered that they can record, press and distribute their own cassettes and CDs by mail and small outlets, doing a complete end-run around the big record companies. In less developed countries, bands and small labels can still get their music out through distributors and importers like Africassette in Detroit, Rashid's in New York and Hatikvah in Los Angeles (see reviews on page 133).

This music chapter is divided into six smaller sections. The first three sections contain reviews of individual recordings; the sections are Independent (or Indy) Music, New Music and World Music. Indy recordings are mostly homebrew affairs, some by a single person working in his or her garage; others are recorded and released by small, regional labels. The styles of Indy Music range from pure noise to melodic pop to rock to weirdly experimental. The World Music section covers mostly non-Western/European recordings, both alternative and traditional. New Music, as a category, is a mystery to most people. This section contains mostly modern recordings that straddle boundaries; on a single disc or tape (or song), you might hear elements of classical, jazz, rock, World Music, electronic and folk.

Along with each recording, you'll find the name of its label. If the recording is from a small or hard-to-find label, there's ordering information.

Following the record reviews, are sections listing a wide range of excellent music books and zines. The last section is a directory of record distributors and importers that, between them, can get you just about any type of music, from Inuit folk songs to industrial recordings so nasty they could drop an Airedale at thirty yards.

The Aerial

$30/year (4 cassettes); $45/year (4 CDs); overseas $55 CD; $40 cassettes) ppd from: The Nonsequitur Foundation, P.O. Box 2638, Santa Fe, NM 87504; 505/986-0004

A quarterly sound magazine of new and experimental music. You'll find a variety of styles here, from acoustic folk-inspired songs to ambient electronics, grating mechanical drones to ethereal vocals. Some of the artists included in the first three Aerial discs are Jeff Greinke, Sue Ann Harkey, Ellen Fullman, Nicolas Collins, Jin Hi Kim, and Richard Kostelanetz. Each disk also includes a beautiful booklet with information on each artist.

Another interesting point: The Aerial is the only journal/recording enterprise I know of that goes out of its way to balance the works of male and female artists. With issue three they hit exactly 50/50, and it's their best issue yet (so fuck you, Camille Paglia).

After Dinner: Editions

$16.50 ppd from: Wayside Music, P.O Box 8427, Silver Spring, MD 20907

It's difficult to talk about Japanese bands without comparing them to bands from the West, since so much of Japanese pop culture is a fairly direct transferal of style eastward. In this context, After Dinner is sort of the Japanese incarnation of Henry Cow; even singer Haco's vocals mimic Dagmar Krause's atonal urgency, but with a precision of expression that is very Japanese. Is it a bad thing to be the new Henry Cow? Maybe not. Henry Cow was daring and ambitious. And After Dinner doesn't just replay the older band's moves, but expands on their ideas, leaving Henry Cow's Marxism behind in favor of a more intimate and technologically sophisticated approach.

Arcane Device: Trout

$15.95 ppd (CA residents add sales tax) from: Silent Records, 540 Alabama St., # 315, San Francisco, CA 94110; cassettes from: Arcane Device, c/o D. Myers, 228 Bleecker St., #8, New York, NY 10014-4420

Arcane Device has been exploring an area of sound that most musicians try desperately to avoid: feedback—pure white noise, con-

trolled and guided down strange pathways. At times, Arcane Device's noise-derived tones remind you of a flute or a violin; at other times, it's like listening to all the world's satellite dishes having a simultaneous nervous breakdown. Challenging and unique—you haven't heard anything like it.

Also recommended: The Feedback Music; Diabolis Ex Machina; Fetish

Black Tape for a Blue Girl: Ashes in the Brittle Air

Cassette $9; CD $15 ppd from: Projekt, P.O. Box 1591, Garden Grove, CA 92642-1591; fax 213-344-0889

Black Tape For A Blue Girl is a hidden treasure of a band. Their sound is lush, full and beautiful, which is not to say wimpy. Ashes in the Brittle Air is beauty with an edge—intense, with an air of longing, like recent Dead Can Dance or Cocteau Twins.

Also recommended: Terrace of Memories; A Chaos of Desire; This Lush Garden Within

Blazing Redheads: Crazed Women

CD $16.98; LP $16.98 ppd (CA residents add sales tax) from: Reference Recordings, P.O. Box 77225X, San Francisco, CA 94107; 800-336-8866

Screaming hot sax-heavy jazz propelled along by tasty Afro-Latin percussion. What really sets the Blazing Redheads apart from a lot of others bands is that the band is blessed with a wealth of composing talent that includes all four of the Redheads' core players. This opens up their sound considerably, since each composer has a slightly different approach. Highlights include Alto sax player Donna Viscuso's opening tribute to Dollar Brand, tenor player Klaudia Promessi's jumpy "Loss of Logic" and percussionist Michaelle Goerlitz's smooth "Cosmo."

This is one band that definitely deserves more fame and fortune than they've received. The album is here; the band's done its part. Now all you have to do is yours—get out those checkbooks....

Also recommended: Blazing Redheads

Botanica: Gardens of Earthly Delights

$14 ppd (CA residents add sales tax) from: Coriolis Records, P.O. Box 3528, Orange, CA 92665

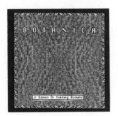

Run a damp finger around the edge of a crystal wineglass. Hear it sing? Take a violin bow, one infinitely long and made of light, and a fractal. Like the glass, you can play the fractal, running the bow along its bifurcated edge, like a musical saw whose tiny shark teeth are microscopic musical saws holding still smaller saws.... Botanica's music sounds the way a fractal looks: complex, fractured, utterly mysterious.

Also recommended: Strange Attractor

Brave Combo:
No, No, No, Cha, Cha, Cha

$16.50 ppd from: Rounder Records, One Camp Street, Cambridge, MA 02140

Brave Combo is sort of a musical reclamation society, playing tunes and styles you probably grew up making fun of—polkas, salsa, waltzes, cha chas, etc. Their impulse toward redemption (and satire) is enhanced by their fluid playing abilities. How many bands do you know of that can play the Rolling Stones' "Satisfaction" as a cha cha and make it work? Brave Combo does on one of this disc's high conceptual points. All of their recordings are recommended, combining cut-out bin sensibilities with first-rate musicianship in an insane stew that is much more than the sum of its parts.

Also recommended: A Night on Earth; Polkatharsis; Humansville; Musical Varieties

Cassette Mythos Audio Alchemy

Cassette $9.50; CD $13.50; Book: Cassette Mythos ed. by Robin James $13.50; Cassette & book $21; CD & book $25 ppd from: The Nonsequitur Foundation, P.O. Box 2638, Santa Fe, NM 87504; 505/986-0004

A document of the "cassette conspiracy" indy art scene. Back in the mid-80s *Op* magazine (later *Option*, see review on page 131) was reviewing indy cassettes just like releases from the big record companies. No one had ever taken this garage and bedroom product seriously before, and some terrific recordings and genuinely talented people surfaced due to their exposure in *Op. Option* no longer reviews indy cassettes with the same enthusiasm, but the scene is still out there; some members have adapted to new environments by moving to indy CD production, but cassettes are still the main means of communication among the various indy tribes. This CD collects tunes, noises and performances by some of the seminal cassette artists in the scene. There is also a book, **Cassette Mythos**, that complements the recording; the book contains info and comments from many more musicians than the few sampled here, and is recommended to anyone looking to get a handle on a unique (and mostly ignored) musical movement.

Michael Chocholak: Blood Music

Cassette $8 ppd from: M&M Music, Route 1, Box 55, Cove, OR 97824

A staunch non-MIDI user, Chocholak collects sound samples from rural Oregon, trips to urban areas and from whacking whatever objects he finds lying around; he then manipulates them, a sound at a time, through a battery of effects devices until they groan or sing the way he wants them to. The resulting tapes vary widely, covering styles from soothing New Age washes, to frightening industrial assaults, to demented rock. It was for releases like these that home taping was invented.

Also recommended: **All Fire's The Fire**; **Red Spider, White Web**; Das Devonian Tag

Robin Crutchfield: Darkest Before Dawn

$13.50 ppd from: Robin Crutchfield, 231 Thompson Street, Box 12, New York, NY 10012

Gothic without the oppression; precise without pickiness. Former DNA keyboardist Crutchfield provides mood music for a church that might actually have something interesting to say.

Angel Corpus Christi: The 80s

Cassette $8; CD $8 ppd (make checks payable to A&R/Ent) from: A&R/Ent, P.O. Box 22113, San Francisco, CA 94122

An accordion-wielding chanteuse who sings not only eccentric and heartfelt original tunes, but covers everything from Alice Cooper's "Eighteen" to Richard Hell's "Blank Generation" to a Bernard Herrmann medley from the film "Taxi Driver." In lesser hands this material might come across as camp or pretentious, but Angel Corpus Christi's sound is so simple and intelligent, and her crooner's voice so perfectly suited to the material that you soon forget that "Blank Generation" was originally squealed and screamed, not whispered, as in her version. And all of the original songs are fine things, including the lament for a dead actor in "John Cassavetes," and a hidden pop-gem, "Hell." Suicide's Alan Vega provides guest vocals on "Dream Baby Dream."

Also recommended: Accordion Pop Vol. 1; Dim the Lights

Nicolas Collins:
It Was a Dark and Stormy Night

$15 ppd (NY, CT and NJ residents add sales tax) from: Trace Element Records, 172 E. 4th St., Ste. 11D, New York, NY 10009

Nicolas Collins' work is barely music at all; it is closer to what the composer Edgard Varese called "controlled noise." In his own distinctive way, what Collins does is similar to many dub and rap artists: he uses modern technology to manipulate the character of music that already exists. In his previous albums, Collins has taken the sounds of easy listening and dance music and by running them through his battery of delays and computer controls, he cuts and splices the music into something extremely uneasy and non-danceable.

On It Was a Dark and Stormy Night, he applies the same cut-and-splice principles to fractured real-time duets with the Soldier String Quartet, schizophrenic reinterpretations of Peruvian brass music, and the title work, his most ambitious experiment to date, a combination of his electronic fetishism with live performers and acoustic instruments.

Also recommended: 100 of the World's Most Beautiful Melodies

D'Cuckoo

Cassette $10 ($15 foreign); CD $15 ($21 foreign) ppd (CA residents add sales tax) from: D'Cuckoo International, Inc., 6114 La Salle Ave., # 414, Oakland, CA 94611; info hotline 510-869-4618

The first full-length release from a bunch of talented women that stomp the line between techno and tribal like nobody's business. D'Cuckoo's lyrics are earnest, New Agey and heartfelt, and the weakest part of the recording. When they cut loose and just play their homemade MIDI percussion, however, they are thrilling. One unexpected treat on the album is their remarkable cover of Eno's "No One Receiving," in which they completely rework the tune into something utterly new and uniquely their own. It alone is worth the price of the disc.

By the time you read this, they ought to have wrapped up their performance video. That and other D'Cuckoo momentos (such as T-shirts and bike shorts) are also available from D'Cuckoo International.

Djam Karet: Suspension and Displacement

$14.50 ppd (CA residents add sales tax) from: Djam Karet/HC Productions, P.O. Box 883, Claremont, CA 91711

Imagine a psychedelic King Crimson and you'll have some idea of Djam Karet's sound. In a ballsy move for a small indy outfit, they've released two new CDs simultaneously. **Burning the Hard City** continues the peel-the-paint-off-the-walls-with-sound tradition of DK's **Reflections from the Firepool** album; **Suspension and Displacement** is the the real gem here, though, a seamless collection of ambient atmospherics functioning as sort of the aural equivalent of postmodern architecture.

Also recommended: **The Ritual Continues**

Julie Frith: Music for Restaurants

Cassette $8 ppd from: Ladd-Frith, P.O. Box 967, Eureka, CA 95502

A restaurant with crystal chandeliers and lace tablecloths. The paté is excellent. But why do all the waiters have heads like insects, and why are they all walking backwards? They must be listening to Julie Frith's **Music for Restaurants**: mood music for the slightly deranged.

Zuzaan Kali Fasteau: Worlds Beyond Words

Cassette $12; CD $18 ppd (make checks payable to Zuzaan Kali Fasteau) from: Flying Note Records, P.O. Box 1027, New York, NY 10013-0865

Calling Fasteau a "composer and multi-instrumentalist" is kind of like calling Einstein "a clever little guy." Fasteau's loose, world-jazz sound is infused with myriad influences picked up on her world travels; while learning some of the local styles, she expanded her sound to include such non-Western instruments as North Africa's *ney* flute and *mizmar*, as well as the Japanese *shakuhachi*.The unusual mix of instruments aside, it's ultimately Fasteau herself that makes this release special. Her utter ease with the music is the artist's loss of ego, where the music takes over and plays itself.

Also recommended: **Prophecy**; **Affinity**; **Beyond Words**; **Bliss**

Jeff Greinke: In Another Place

$15.95 ppd ($16.95 Canada) from: Linden Music, P.O. Box 520, Linden, VA 22642

If Greinke were a painter, he'd be doing landscapes. His solo (and occasionally collaborative) electronic recordings move seamlessly from the fog-laden ambient rainforests to more urgent and edgy cityscapes. Echoes of Eastern and even stripped down folk-forms bubble up like magma from a deep fissure. A subtle recording of dark and spacious sounds.

Also recommended: **Changing Skies**; **Crossing Ngoli**; **Lost Terrain**

The Hub

$17 ppd (NY residents add sales tax) from: Cadence, Cadence Bldg., Redwood, NY 13679; 315-287-2852

THE HUB
Computer Network Music

What do you do when you want to jam with a bunch of synthesizer players, but none of your machines are compatible? You build the Hub, a sort of neutral zone, where all your sounds can get together and interact electronically. The music is reminiscent of Stockhausen and the Princeton/Columbia electronic music labs.

King Crimson: The Great Deceiver

Caroline Records

The Great Deceiver is a four-CD set that captures King Crimson in their natural environment—playing live to an attentive audience. The dates range from 1973 to '74 when Crimson was in one of its strongest incarnations, consisting of Robert Fripp, Bill Bruford, John Wetton and David Cross. Both the level of writing and of musicianship here is nothing short of amazing; that any individual, let alone group, could keep together the complex polyrhythms that are the basis for such Crimson classics as "Larks' Tongue in Aspic" and "The Talking Drum," is inspiring. The booklet that accompanies the discs contains Crimson photos from the period, as well as reviews and excerpts from Fripp's road journals.

Master/Slave Relationship: Being Led Around by the Tongue

Cassette $10; CD $15 ppd from: Master/Slave Relationship, P.O. Box 191211, San Francisco, CA 94119-1211

Tough, erotic, poetic, driving. Debbie Jaffe (M/SR's brains) writes and plays music that explores power games and sex roles. Jaffe's work is in the same vein as other uncompromising contemporary women artists, such as Kathy Acker and Lydia Lunch. M/SR aren't afraid to go into forbidden or dangerous territory, and they invite you to join them.

Also recommended: A New Explanation for Decadence

Mo Boma: Jijimuge

$18 ppd (make checks payable to David Hodgson) from: Playing by Ear, 1244 Mojave Dr., Colton, CA 92324; 909-824-8749

Imagine if that gold-plated record in the Voyager probe ever gets picked up by aliens who figure out how to play it, but don't really pick up on the fact that the different musical styles are in fact supposed to be different. Mo Boma produces the late tech sort of digital primitive sound that someone from another planet might call world music. And they'd be right.

The Molecules: Steel Toe

Information from: Tragic Mule, 4001 San Leandro Street, # 7, Oakland, CA 94601

You're walking down a dark, damp street, just minding your own business. Suddenly Captain Beefheart and Joey Ramone jump out of the shadows and beat the crap out of you while singing the theme from "The Flintstones." It hurts, but it sounds great. You tip big.

Mondo Vanilli

Cassette $12 ppd (make checks payable to Ken Goffman) from: R.U. Sirius, c/o M. Vanilli, P.O. Box 10171, Berkeley, CA 94709-0171

Cyber-laced hip-hop for the smart drugs crowd, produced by and starring R.U. Sirius with other good folks at the hyper-culture zine *Mondo 2000*. This tape is big fun for exactly the same reasons as the magazine—it's flashy, with a high-definition gloss and a heavy silliness factor, and done with such honest idiot glee that you'd have to have a rather enormous stick up your ass not to love it.

The Muffins: Chronometers

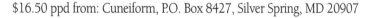

$16.50 ppd from: Cuneiform, P.O. Box 8427, Silver Spring, MD 20907

Combining elements of free jazz, New Music and rock & roll, The Muffins were one of smartest and most capable bands of the 70s. Naturally, they never rose above cult status. Now over an hour of their best material has been beautifully remastered on CD by studio wizard Kit Watkins. The numbers range from a 20-minute-plus title track to intricate barely-more-than-a-minute jazz ruminations.

Nightcrawlers: Barriers

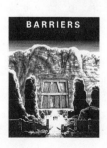

$15 ppd from: Peter Gulch, 1493 Greenwood Ave., Camden, NJ 08103

The Nightcrawlers started out a decade ago as kind of a low-rent Americanized Tangerine Dream. Now that their Teutonic forebearers are lost in the land of New Age junk food, the Nightcrawlers have become a force all on their own. They answer the question: What if those German synth bands from the 70s hadn't softened and gone pulpy, like Dali watches left out in the sun?

PGR: The Chemical Bride

$15.95 ppd (CA residents add sales tax) from: Silent Records, 540 Alabama St., Ste. 315, San Francisco, CA 94110

PGR has never been about traditional music so much as sound exploration. Think of Mark Rothko's nearly monochromatic canvases; at first all you see is a single mass of color. But, as you look longer the subtleties emerge—changes in texture, in hue and color. That's the sound of PGR's music. At first it's a wall, and then it's the cracks in the wall, and then it's the fractal patterns of the smallest details at the wall/crack interface.

Also recommended: GRAV; Fetish

Phew

$19 ppd (CA residents add sales tax) from: Silent Records, 540 Alabama St., Ste. 315, San Francisco, CA 94110

German electronics and world beat experiments collide like crazed particles in a supercollider when three-quarters of Germany's Can play back-up for Japanese vocalist Phew. The band is cool and cerebral, a glistening Teutonic Karaoke wetdream. Phew's atonal vocals are harsh by contrast, though her voice is warm and comely. The juxtaposition of sounds is startling and memorable, like wearing a fiberglass tuxedo.

Richard Pinhas: East/West

$18.50 ppd from: Cuneiform, P.O. Box 8427, Silver Spring, MD 20907

If you don't know who Richard Pinhas is, don't feel bad. As a rule, it's wise to ignore French rock musicians because they usually stink on ice, and you will feel so bad you'll want to hold a telethon. Pinhas, however, is the exception that proves the rule. His band, Heldon, could scorch with the best of the progressive bands. The closest analog to their sound was early King Crimson. East/West, a post-Heldon solo album, continues in that tradition. With its driving synths and razor blade guitar, East/West remains powerful eleven years after its initial release.

Also recommended: DWW; L'Ethique; Iceland; Interface; Allez Teia

Vicki Richards: Parting the Waters

Cassette $9; CD $15 ppd from: Projekt, P.O. Box 1591, Garden Grove, CA 92642-1591

If this tape were on a major label with a big ad budget, you would already know Vicki Richards' name because she would be a star. Mining an area of sound somewhere between world music and jazz (think of Glen Velez or Jon Hassell's work), Richards and her excellent backing band shimmer, bow and drum their way through tunes that will make you think of South America one minute, then Africa, then the Caribbean, and the Middle East.

Also recommended: Quiet Touch

Peter Van Riper: Acoustic Metal Music

Cassette $7 ppd from: Peter Van Riper, 73 Calyer Street, Brooklyn, NY 11222

Tibetans use common objects—brass bowls—as musical instruments, striking and rubbing them to produce pure gong-like tones for meditation, prayer, and pleasure. Peter Van Riper discovered in common Western objects—aluminum baseball bats—the same thing that the Tibetans discovered in their bowls: a cheap source of magical sounds right under his nose. Or home plate, or something. The sounds move from ambient standing waves to dynamic gamelan sounds.

Also recommended: Direct Contact; Sound to Movement; Room Space

Clara Rockmore: The Art of the Theremin

Delos International

Decades before the theremin was relegated to the soundtracks of bad 50s SF potboilers, it was considered a serious electronic musical instrument, producing a sound somewhere between a violin and a human voice, but much weirder than either. During its brief heyday in the 30s, the only official theremin virtuoso was Clara Rockmore, performing stock still, a single tomb-like speaker/monitor behind her, like some Bauhaus Madonna. On her only recording, Clara performs classical tunes by Stravinsky, Tchaikovsky, Saint-Saens, and others, accompanied by her sister on the piano.

Rotodoti: Tarzan Speaks

$17 ppd (NY residents add sales tax) from: Cadence, Cadence Bldg., Redwood, NY 13679; 315-287-2852; Plate Technophonics; cassette $10 ppd from: Tom Nunn, 3016 25th St., San Francisco, CA 94110; The Well Deconstructed Cello; cassette $10 ppd from: Doug Carroll, 3127A Mission St., San Francisco, CA 94110

Like the soundtrack to a nervous breakdown, Rotodoti is an improv group that blends together computer noise, cello, trombone and Tom Nunn's homemade percussion into a moody, jittery homebrew bound to leave you looking for something to whack, strum, squeeze or blow into so that you won't feel left out of the process. Not for the anxious or Michael Bolton fans.

Also recommended are solo cassettes from percussionist Tom Nunn and cellist Doug Carroll. Nunn's tape consists of solo percussion on his homemade instruments. Carroll's tape is an exercise in extended technique and abuse of his cello, in which he coaxes sounds both organic and inorganic from its body.

The Shaggs

$16.50 ppd from: Rounder Records, One Camp Street, Cambridge, MA 02140

There are places in Nepal where they constantly re-invent Western cooking from photos. For instance, north of Kathmandu if you order pizza, you will get a chapati topped with ketchup and yak cheese. The Shaggs were three nice suburban girls who played pop music they way Nepalis cook pizzas—as if they had only seen pictures of guitars and drums and guessed at what they would sound like.

The Shaggs' sound is unearthly, at once utterly stupid and frighteningly avant garde. No other band has ever come so close to capturing the sparse, grating, harrowing sound of the early Velvet Underground—and the Shaggs weren't even trying. They wanted to be Karen Carpenter. This CD includes all the songs from their two vinyl albums, plus unreleased material.

Elliot Sharp & Carbon: Tocsin

Enemy Productions

When I say that Elliot Sharp & Carbon have released their second commercial album (**Datacide** being the first) remember that it's a little like saying that *Naked Lunch*, the film, is nicer than **Naked Lunch**, the book. Sharp and Carbon's music is as complex, noiseful and dangerous as ever; imagine funky speed metal played by a bunch of physics majors on crack.

Also recommended: **Datacide**; Beneath the Valley of the Ultra-Yahoos

The Stiff Records Box Set

$51 ppd (CA residents add sales tax) from: Rhino Records, 2225 Colorado Ave., Santa Monica, CA 90404-3555

In the late 70s and early 80s, Stiff Records created a whole culture around itself by producing and distributing some of the best non-big label acts in England. This four-disc set is a collection of terrific songs, but it also captures an exciting, hopeful moment in time. Nice, though minimal, notes and packaging. Featured performers include Parker, The Pogues, Madness, Nick Lowe, Elvis Costello, The Damned and Ian Drury, and a host of others.

David Sylvian & Russell Mills: Ember Glance

Venture/Caroline

A book-and-CD set documenting an environmental art space that included sound, light and sculpture, constructed by David Sylvian and Russell Mills. The book contains not only photos of the art as it appeared in the show, but also production notes, sketches and shots of the environment under construction. The final piece is like some natural history museum gone mad, with organic shapes slipping from the frames and boxes onto the walls and floor; it's a space that seems to have grown in place, rather than been constructed. The accompanying CD is quite minimal and functional in the context of the show (but is lovely to listen to on its own), an ambient mixture of large soft structures, with occasional stabs of voice and metallic tones, not unlike Sylvian's recent recordings with Holger Czukay.

Kit Watkins: Thought Tones, Vol. 1

$15.95 ppd ($16.95 Canada) from: Linden Music, P.O. Box 520, Linden, VA 22642

Music as pure sound. Sound as landscape, an environment that encloses you. No melodies here, just *thought tones*, aural oases that allow your imagination to wander where it wants, or demands.

If you heard and liked Volume One, you'll like Two. They're complementary releases, similar in idea and method, but different enough to remain distinct works.

Also recommended: **wet, dark and low**; Circle

Carl Weingarten: Pandora's Garage

$15.95 ppd ($16.95 Canada) from: Linden Music, P.O. Box 520, Linden, VA 22642

Guitarist Carl Weingarten is one of the truly great indy musicians working today. **Pandora's Garage** is sort of fake movie music for films that don't exist. Each cut is like a micro story, creating a mood, or whisking you off to some intriguing place. Highlights include "Two Half Moons," with Walter Whitney's languorous trumpet lines, and the atmospheric opening cut, "Prelude to Pandora."

Also recommended: **Primitive Earth**; Laughing at Paradise; Slide of Hand

Pamela Z: Echolocation

Cassette $8 ppd (make checks payable to Pamela Z) from: ZED, 1181 Valencia St., San Francisco, CA 94110

Echolocation, by San Francisco avant-Diva Pamela Z, uses simple techniques such as multiple delay lines and multi-tracking to create lustrous sonic landscapes using only Ms. Z's astonishingly well-trained vocal cords. There are even a couple of more traditionally song-ish pieces thrown in, with drums and a catchy hook and everything. But the star here isn't the playing or the effects, but Pamela Z's lovely voice itself.

a produce: reflect like a mirror, respond like an echo

$14.50 ppd from: Trance Port, P.O. Box 85436, Los Angeles, CA 90072

Ambient, spacious compositions, combining electronic sensibilities with fourth-world timbres and atmosphere. The title tune features Ruben Garcia's melodic treated piano lines. Chas Smith's steel guitar adds an ominous undercurrent to "Rousseau's Jungle." Even the packaging, a unique folded paper cover, is special. This album is for anyone who thinks the ambient genre is dried up.

David Behrman: Unforeseen Events

$15 ppd from: Experimental Intermedia Foundation, 224 Centre Street, New York, NY 10013

David Behrman is a very twentieth-century composer in that he doesn't write scores for musicians to perform, but creates software for musicians to interact with. Unforeseen Events is a short quartet of pieces built around the playing style of Ben Neill and his three-belled "mutantrumpet." The timbres and phrases Behrman's software extracts from Neill's input is both subtle and truly complementary. Three other short pieces, built around the idea of overlapping and interweaving sustained notes, round out this inventive disc.

David Borden: The Continuing Story of Counterpoint, Parts 1-4 + 8

$16.50 ppd from: Cuneiform, P.O. Box 8427, Silver Spring, MD 20907

With his ensemble, Borden practices a kind of minimalism that moves in the opposite direction of, say, Philip Glass. You could even call Borden's style maximalist to describe the Phil Specter-like wall-of-sound produced by his kinetic, looping melody lines. In fact, Borden's music has less in common with modern minimalists, and a lot more with the kind of heavy counterpoint and contra-puntal tendencies found in Baroque music. Imagine an updating of the Bach "Inventions" played by denizens from the New York downtown art scene.

Glenn Branca: Symphony No. 6 (Devil Choirs at the Gates of Heaven)

$15.95 ppd (CA residents add sales tax) from: Silent Records, 540 Alabama St., # 315, San Francisco, CA 94110

Musicians have been trying to blend the violent sonics of rock with the structure of classical music for the last twenty years. The results have been lame for the most part, resulting in little more than the baroque molasses of bands like Yes and the hysterical pomp of Emerson, Lake and Palmer.

Someone who has made the rock/classical connection work is Glenn Branca. Through a series of increasingly dense works, he's explored his fascination with both drones and the harmonic overtone series. Branca combines batteries of custom-made electric guitars chording over simple drum patterns that simultaneously echo Black Flag and Stravinsky. **Symphony No. 6 (Devil Choirs at the Gates of Heaven)** was commissioned by the Massachusetts Council for the Arts, and it's probably Branca's best work to date. The percussion is primitive, pounding out the rhythms of some weird urban tribalism. **Symphony No. 6** drives like the best rock & roll, but is controlled, heightening the tension of the music. The dense mix of closely tuned guitars fools your ears, convincing you that you're hearing a much larger ensemble, even other instruments like brass, violins and cellos.

Also recommended: **Symphony No. 1 (Tonal Plexus)**; **Symphony No.2 (The Peak of the Sacred)**; **The World Upside Down**

Michael Brook: Cobalt Blue

4AD/Warner

Solo outings by session guitarists are mostly like visits to the dentist: occasionally to be endured, but seldom enjoyed. **Cobalt Blue**, however, is the exception that proves the rule. The tune "Red Shift" is an ultralight buzz over a 21st-century Riyadh, while "Hawaii" burns quietly, like the sun coming up over the rim of a dormant volcano. Brook's first solo record, **Hybrid**, is also exceptional, and heavily influenced by producer Brian Eno's ambient sound.

Gavin Bryars:
Three Viennese Dancers

ECM New Series

While researching text for an aria to be sung by the character Mata Hari in another composer's opera, Gavin Bryars discovered something interesting: one night in Vienna in late 1906, the three most famous dancers of the day (Mata Hari, Maud Allan and Isadora Duncan) were staying in hotels, all unaware of each other's presence.

When the Mata Hari scene was dropped from the opera, Bryars reworked the piece, substituting French horn for the voice. This became the first Viennese dance, and is important because it points out the fact that unlike ordinary dance music that's highly rhythmic, Bryars' music is more lyrical and atmospheric. Which isn't to say it's not rhythmic; the predominant sound on the recording is a gamelan-like tuned percussion. The emphasis, however, is more impressionistic. Bryars doesn't so much establish a beat to represent the three dancers, but rather creates a sound background through which his (and our) images of the dancers can move. A lovely and surprising recording.

Also recommended: Hommages; The Sinking of the Titanic; After the Requiem

Paul Dresher:
Dark Blue Circumstance

$17 ppd (CA residents add sales tax) from: New Albion Records, 584 Castro Street, #515, San Francisco, CA 94114

Sinuous, obsessive lines of overdubbed guitar from Dresher's custom delay system create a metallic waterfall of sound. You've probably heard similar delay/overdubbing pieces before, but few players can match Dresher's control or melody sense. Also on the disc are three ensemble pieces that combine elements of Western, Far Eastern and African compositions. A highlight is the haunting "Night Songs;" scored for singers and chamber orchestra, it brings together Native American, African and Polynesian texts on waking, sleeping and dreaming.

Robert Een & Dale Edwin Newton: Music from the Blue Earth

$15 ppd from: Blue Earth Records, 520 E., 12th St., #6B, New York, NY 10009

What Hendrix did for the guitar, freeing it from its previous musical roles and expectations, Robert Een and Dale Edwin Newton attempt for the cello. And for the most part, they succeed on **Music from the Blue Earth**. Multi-tracking themselves, Een and Newton create numerous cello groupings, from quartets to whole ensembles. While keeping on eye on their classical roots, Een and Newton's sound moves from modern popish airs to Bartok and minimalism.

Morton Feldman: Three Voices for Joan LaBarbara

$17 ppd (CA residents add sales tax) from: New Albion Records, 584 Castro Street, #515, San Francisco, CA 94114

While he was alive, composer Morton Feldman's music was success-fully ignored by just abut everybody. He was known in small New Music circles and influenced many young composers, but his work was performed very little and his recordings are almost non-existent. Since his death in 1987, however, there has been a whole new inter-est in his spare, atmospheric compositions.

A few years before his death, he wrote a solo piece for his friend and vocalist-extraordinaire, Joan LaBarbara. Ironically, the piece was inspired by the death of another friend, the painter Philip Guston: "I saw the piece with Joan in front and these two loudspeakers behind her. There is something tombstoney about the look of loudspeak-ers." The piece is a setting for a poem called "Wind," by Frank O'Hara. In this recording, LaBarbara's multi-tracked voice forms a haunting one-woman ensemble as she sings the lonely poem about snow, loss and evil. Joan LaBarbara is one of the premier New Music vocalists, with a voice as strong as it is beautiful. This simple album is a showcase, not only for her voice, but for the work of a sadly neglected American composer.

Also recommended: **Rothko Chapel/Why Patterns?**; **Triadic Memories**

Fast Forward: Panhandling

Lovely Music

Fast Forward performs sort of the aural equivalent of Rauschenberg's art—he finds stuff, takes it home, messes with it, and makes it into art. In Fast Forward's case, he is a percussionist, so he whacks the stuff with hands, mallets, sticks, and then maybe combines it with other stuff he's found. "Precious Metals" from **Panhandling** is performed partly on his "metal snake," a piece of coiled flat metal he found while walking home one night. The sound matches the name—slinky and wiggly—like a percussive slide whistle. One of the pleasures of FF's music is the mixture of old sounds, such as timbales and tamboura, with brand new sounds.

Lou Harrison:
The Music of Lou Harrison

$18.49 ppd (NY residents add sales tax) from: CRI, Composers Recordings Inc., 170 W. 74th St., New York, NY 10023

Harrison, an old crony of John Cage, is one of the more charming and accessible composers now working. Like Cage, his big artistic breakthrough came when he abandoned the equal tempered scale and started absorbing gamelan music from Bali and Java. It's his tasteful mixture of Western and non-Western scales and sound sources that makes his music so compelling. "Concerto in Slendro" is a violin concerto played over a gamelan-like backing band made up of celeste and prepared pianos. There are two more marginally traditional gamelan pieces on the album, as well as a work-out by the Kronos Quartet on Harrison's "String Quartet Set," the most Western-grounded piece on the disc. A delightful collection of works by a master composer.

Also recommended: **La Koro Sutro**; **Pacifika Rondo & Other Works**; **The Perilous Chapel**

Alan Hovhaness: Visionary Landscapes

$18.48 ppd (CA residents add sales tax) from: Backroads, 417 Tamal Plaza, Corte Madera, CA 94925; 800-825-4848

Like Lou Harrison, Hovhaness' main musical touchpoint is non-Western musics. Unlike Harrison, however, he has largely worked in the traditional equal tempered scale system. This collection of solo piano works shows off his compositional prowess, and understanding of world musics. We hear strains, and sometimes straight transcriptions, of Indian, Armenian, Persian, Arabic and Japanese musics. Particularly lovely are the opening suite, with the first movement's simple pentatonic melody, and "Two Ghazals," transcriptions of Persian love poems.

Brenda Hutchinson: Seldom Still

Cassette $11 ppd ($16 foreign; NY residents add sales tax) from: Deep Listening, Pauline Oliveros Foundation, 156 Hunter Street, Kingston, NY 12401; fax 914-338-5986

On the title piece, a Thai animal call becomes the voice that leads you through a landscape of loss and the death of loved ones. Later, sampled and looped voices of street people, particularly older women, lost voices that few will listen to, talk of their lives, noted, at least on tape. Touchy material, all of this, the kind of thing that could turn easily into parody or insult. In Hutchinson's hands, it does neither, but remains powerful, humane and starkly beautiful.

Lucia Hwong: House of Sleeping Beauties

Private Music

Combining elements of minimalism, jazz and traditional Chinese music, Hwong creates an East/West New Music hybrid that's tense and graceful at the same time. Hwong frequently combines Western instruments such as saxes and synthesizers with Eastern *pipas* and *shakuhachis*. The disc's opening "Tibet Suite," moves subtly from tense ensemble interplay to a melancholy *shakuhachi* solo.

David Hykes & the Harmonic Choir: Hearing Solar Winds

$21.48 ppd (CA residents add sales tax) from: Backroads, 417 Tamal Plaza, Corte Madera, CA 94925; 800-825-4848

David Hykes and company are practitioners of overtone singing, an ancient vocal process that uses the head as a resonating device, like the body of a guitar or the soundboard of a piano. By carefully controlled breathing and throat manipulations, Hykes and the Harmonic Choir extend their vocal range in dazzling ways, highlighting the often-suppressed overtones latent in all human voices.

The result is difficult to describe. It's the sound of time passing, like echoes of echoes of echoes of all the choirs that have ever sung in all the churches of the world. There is simply nothing else like it.

Jin Hi Kim: No World (Trio) Improvisations

Cassette $9.50; CD $16.50 ppd from: O.O. Discs, 502 Anton St., Bridgeport, CT 06606-2121

Kim plays the *komungo*, a fourth-century six-string Korean zither. Its sound is rather like a plucked double bass, but more more mysterious, full of strange timbres and overtones.

The improvs on this disc are what composer Pauline Oliveros means by "deep listening"—improvisation that's not noise and chaos and wild displays of chops, but intense interest in what the other players are up to. On these three-person improvs, Kim and her komungo are accompanied, in various combinations, by didgeridoo, English horn (sans reed), voice, synthesizer, violin, oboe and African percussion instruments. Listen closely and you'll realize the "No World" of the title doesn't just mean the world of instruments, but opening yourself up to the whole world of available sound.

Also recommended: No World Improvisations; Sargeng

Guy Klucevsek: Flying Vegetables of the Apocalypse

$15 ppd from: Experimental Intermedia Foundation, 224 Centre Street, New York, NY 10013

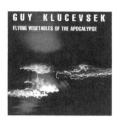

Guy Klucevsek answers the musical question, "Can a talented, young deconstructionist play the accordion?"

Flying Vegetables of the Apocalypse is an inspired showcase of Klucevsek's deceptively simple compositions. The opening tune, "Union Hall," on the surface sounds like a rather straightforward mid-temper dance tune, suitable for an evening at home eating halvah. What's not obvious, however, is that two of the tune's three melodies are Madagascan, and the third is a Slavic dance played in 7/8 time.

Also recommended: Manhattan Cascade

Tod Machover: Flora

Bridge Records

"Computer music" is mostly a dull-as-a-rock affair where academics who can't play make music you can't listen to. Composer and techno-wiz Tod Machover flushes out the computer music system with his own brand of digital enema, by creating music on "hyper-instruments." In Machover's hyper-instrument system traditional instruments such as cello, voice and guitar are fed into a computer system, where they are transformed, sometimes slightly, sometimes tremendously. By responding to what they hear, players can call up new set of tones, textures and melodies from the computer, greatly extending the range and aural possibilities of their instruments.

The title piece on Flora stretches, mutates and shatters a single soprano voice into an eerie cloud of Siren voices; "Bug-Mudra" is an intense guitar/percussion free-for-all that screams like the bastard child of Stravinsky and Glenn Branca. Machover's hyper-instruments put back the human element that has always been missing in traditional computer music, and in doing so Machover has almost single-handedly revitalized the field.

Also recommended: Valis; Spectres

Meredith Monk: Book of Days

ECM New Series

Monk's soundtrack to her film of the same name. Like the film, the music here doesn't follow a traditional "narrative line," but is more evocative of feeling and place. And timelessness—that above all. Monk has a shaman's instincts (and a trained technician's skill) for creating sounds that could be brand new, or a thousand years old. As in most of Monk's work, the human voice is the center of attention, though a few keyboards, hurdy-gurdy, and some strings appear from time to time and are gone, like ghosts from some other ritual in the next room. In both her film and soundtrack, Monk wanted to create a feeling of displacement so that the viewer could see (and hear) the world in a fresh way. She has succeeded admirably.

Also recommended: **Turtle Island**; **Dolmen Music**; Our Lady of the Late

Pauline Oliveros: Crone Music

$18.50 ppd ($21 foreign; NY residents add sales tax) from: Deep Listening, Pauline Oliveros Foundation, 156 Hunter Street, Kingston, NY 12401; fax 914-338-5986

On this album, accordionist/composer Pauline Oliveros works her custom-made squeeze box through a series of slowly-evolving works that are more about landscape than traditional musical forms. Her sound is hushed, subterranean, and captivating; her instrument is tuned in the very, very old just intonation system (remember Pythagoras and his crew?). The music is hypnotic, like a rail journey across an infinitely complex and fascinating countryside, one that changes even as you stare at it.

Pauline Oliveros & Stuart Dempster: Deep Listening

$17 ppd (CA residents add sales tax) from: New Albion Records, 584 Castro Street, #515, San Francisco, CA 94114

Improvisation is at the heart of this album. The title explains it all—when you're improvising music, you're listening deeply. Pauline Oliveros, Stuart Dempster and vocalist Panatois are all master listeners and improvisers. On their own, Oliveros and Dempster have

both experimented with extended echoes, both natural and electronically produced. The way instruments come and go in the mix, and extreme reverb gives **Deep Listening** a sense of openness, while the sparse instrumentation gives the music an enclosed feeling. The album sounds as if it were recorded in the dark, somewhere underground. While calm, this music is the antithesis of New Age—Oliveros' just intonation accordion and the subterranean rumble of Dempster's didgeridoo carry too much menace for that.

Also recommended: **The Ready Made Boomerang**; Troglodyte's Delight

Harry Partch: The Bewitched

$18.49 ppd (NY residents add sales tax) from: CRI, Composers Recordings Inc., 170 W. 74th St., New York, NY 10023

Harry Partch was an American musical shaman. When ordinary music could no longer contain his ideas, he went off to the desert and invented his own instruments (many loosely based on Balinese and Javanese percussion), including cloud chamber bowls, the diamond marimba, Chromelodeon and the Zymo-Xyl (cobbled together from hubcaps, a kettletop, oak blocks and old boxes).

Using a homebrew tuning system that divided up the scale into 43 notes instead of the normal twelve-tone Western scale, Partch's compositions often have the wild intensity of a primitive ritual. In fact, in the liner notes for the recording of his theater dance-piece, **The Bewitched,** Partch says, "It is a satyr play. It is a seeking for release—through satire, whimsy, magic, ribaldry—from the catharsis of tragedy."

Also recommended: **The Music of Harry Partch**; Revelation in the Courthouse Park

Maggie Payne: Crystal

Lovely Music

On **Crystal**, Maggie Payne uses studio techniques such as multi-tracking and signal processing, and especially digital delay, to build up pieces from fragments of pre-recorded sound. Multi-tracked voices shift in and out of phase, setting up alternately shimmering and percussive pattens in "White Night;" "Scirocco" uses the digital delays and 32 tracks of flute to create a rainforest where instruments cry to each other like chrome birds; "Crystal" is the soundtrack to a video of growing crystals, and its dense amniotic washes suit its subject well; "Solar Wind" is the most elaborate piece using computer time compression, and heavy signal processing of NASA solar wind recordings from Voyager-2.

Project Ars Nova: The Island of St. Hylarion

$17 ppd (CA residents add sales tax) from: New Albion Records, 584 Castro Street, #515, San Francisco, CA 94114

"Ars Nova" means "New Art," in this case post-14th-century, when the church-dominated chanting was giving way to wacky concepts like rhythm and harmony. Project Ars Nova is an early music group from Boston that specializes in digging up interesting and unusual pre-Baroque tunes. In this case, they stumbled on a set of 15th-century court songs from Cyprus. The rhythms are subtly odd, and the melodies are a more complex and fragile cousin of French (and British) folk music of the period. Project Ars Nova are the punks of the early music scene, searching out lost musical gems, and bringing a sense of excitement and adventure to a form known mostly for its snore-factor.

Also recommended: **Ars Magis Subtiliter**; **Homage to Johannes Ciconia**

Terry Riley: In C

$18.48 ppd (CA residents add sales tax) from: Backroads, 417 Tamal Plaza, Corte Madera, CA 94925; 800-825-4848

Twenty-five years ago, Terry Riley premiered **In C** and gave birth

(and legitimacy) to the whole musical school known as minimalism. This new recording is remarkable for a number of reasons. Recorded in China before Tianemen. Tapes had to be smuggled out of the country. Chinese musicians had never really played Western avant-garde music; their native instruments aren't even tuned in the same scale system.

Steve Roach, David Hudson, Sarah Hopkins: Australia (Sound of the Earth)

$18.48 ppd (CA residents add sales tax) from: Backroads, 417 Tamal Plaza, Corte Madera, CA 94925; 800-825-4848

A collaboration between American synthesist Steve Roach, Australian aborigine musician David Hudson, and composer/performer Sarah Hopkins. This is one of those rare occasions where each performer brings out the best in the others, creating a seamless recording of genuine and subtle power. Roach goes to great lengths to keep his synthesizer a supporting player, laying down a tonal foundation, but never showing off. It's the acoustic instruments—didgeridoo, cello and voice—that dominate. The result is a unique soundscape that lies somewhere between the hissing of the wind across the Outback and the sizzling of circuit boards in an overheating PC.

Stephen Scott: Minerva's Web

$17 ppd (CA residents add sales tax) from: New Albion Records, 584 Castro Street, #515, San Francisco, CA 94114

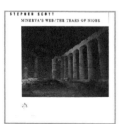

Imagine a piano minus the keys. How do you play it? Easy: crawl inside, you and nine friends. Caress the strings; pluck them, hit them, saw away at them.

Scott and his ensemble take the piano away from the percussion instruments and give it to the strings and voices, coaxing from its sound board noises neither Beethoven nor Thelonius Monk ever dreamed were in there. Cage and others have played inside the piano too, but only Scott has transformed what was a compositional conceit into a truly beautiful musical language.

Chas Smith: Nakadai

LP $11 ppd from: Arc Light Records, 17912 Erwin, Reseda, CA 91335

Chas Smith is a pedal steel guitarist with a difference. Instead of Waylon Jennings-type honky-tonk fills, Smith explores the somnambulistic side of the instrument. The unique properties of the steel guitar, the possibilities for sitar-like resonances and sinuous melody lines, give it a ghostly, almost aquatic sound at times. If the house band on the Titanic sounded this gorgeous when the ship went down, you might have been tempted to stay aboard.

Nakadai's other unique quality is that it's recorded on vinyl. It is not a CD or a tape. You need a regular record player to hear it. If you were silly enough to get rid of your vinyl player when CDs came out, too bad for you. You're missing out on a lot of great foreign and indy music.

Carl Stone: Mom's

$17 ppd (CA residents add sales tax) from: EAM, P.O. Box 38176, Los Angeles CA 90038

Hip-Hop rhythm collages made "sampling" a household word, but they're not the end of the story. Composer Carl Stone uses extended Mac-based sampling techniques to slice and dice found sounds— bits of a Schubert lieder, Zydeco, gamelan, electric guitars—into stuttering cybernetic dances and backbrain ambient landscapes. The opening cut in particular, "Banteay Srey," begins with a breathy descending and ascending melodic line that's looped, delayed and finally joined by a single organ line, giving the tune a sense of openness and space.

Taking an essentially sculptural approach to music, Stone is a master craftsman, making Fabergé eggs out of ones and zeros.

Also recommended: Four Pieces

Margaret Leng Tan: Litania

$17 ppd (CA residents add sales tax) from: New Albion Records, 584 Castro Street, #515, San Francisco, CA 94114

Singapore native Margaret Leng Tan is one of the leading new music pianists now playing. On Litania, she plays the works of Japanese

composer Somei Satoh. Satoh has been influenced by both Shintoism and Zen Buddhism and his music has the stark "internal" quality of both those disciplines.

While using a very European Romantic sound palette, Satoh's music remains very Japanese in that it is less about melody and harmony and more concerned with tonal color. On several pieces he uses digital delays, setting up layers of piano sound, playing similar harmonic parts. The first piece, "The Heavenly Spheres are Illuminated by Lights" featuring soprano Lise Messier, is also the most linear and European, becoming a kind of 20th-century Romanticism.

Also recommended: Sonic Encounters

La Monte Young: The Well-Tuned Piano

Cassettes $55.95; CDs $85.95; LPs $65.95 ppd (NY residents add sales tax) from: MELA Foundation, Inc., 275 Church St., New York, NY 10013

Before there was Philip Glass or Steve Reich, before there was a thing called "minimalism" there was La Monte Young.

Young's most famous, and most accessible, work has also been recently reissued. The Well-Tuned Piano is a five-hour performance/improv for prepared piano. Not only has Young completely rebuilt the guts of his Bosendorfer grand, he's tuned it in the just intonation system. The result is a sound that at times is gamelan-like, and at times almost industrial as weird overtones build up, forming metallic sheets of noise that shouldn't come from a piano. Young's music requires patience and a degree of work, but not more than, say, reading Gravity's Rainbow.

Also recommended: The Second Dream of the High-Tension Line Stepdown Transformer from the Four Dreams of China

3 Mustaphas 3: Shopping

Cassette $9.80; CD $14.80 ppd (NJ residents add sales tax) from: Shanachie Records, 37 E. Clinton St., Newton, NJ 07860; 201-579-7763

The Mustaphas describe their music as "local music—strictly local music—from all over the world." A Balkan-based (Szegarely, specifically) high-spirited, mutantly traditional band, their tunes can sound like an Eastern European march, a belly dancing tune and a Tex-Mex two-step all at the same time. Imagine the coolest ethnic wedding band in the world.

A Luaka Bop: Roots, Rock and Rhythm

Luaka Bop/Reprise

There's probably no better introduction to the popular music of South America and Cuba that the series of discs from David Byrne's Luaka Bop label. Starting with the release of the splashy **Brazil Classics One**, Byrne has ranged all over the region bringing back a fine collection of Brazilian folk forms (**Brazil Classics 3: Forros, Etc.**), and collections of Cuban hits, including recordings of Tom Zé, Silvio Rodriguez and **Diablo al Infierno**, a collection of dance tunes.

Roots, Rock and Rhythm is a collection of Latin-inspired tunes by European and U.S. artists, mixed with songs by the Brazilian and Cuban artists who inspired them. **Roots, Rock and Rhythm** is a terrific jumping off point for anyone just finding their way into Latin music.

Abed Azrie: Aromates

Elektra Nonesuch

Paris-based Syrian singer/songwriter Abed Azrie comes from a traditional Arabic singing style where songs are crooned rather than belted out. The result is an album with a warm, and at times haunting sound. He combines his traditional vocals with very restrained synthesizer washes; the effect is a subtle expansion of Azrie's sound palette, giving him the freedom he wants without ever slopping over into a commercial pop-rai sound.

Ahlam: Revolt Against Reason

$16.95 ppd ($20.95 Canada; New York resident add sales tax) from: Stern's Music U.S., 598 Broadway, 7th Fl., New York, NY 10012

Jeel is a jumping Arabic pop style. It's overtly political; its lyrics are about the troubles of everyday life: poverty, hunger, political violence, etc. The music has overtones of rai, Western pop, folk melodies and even Jamaican dub. On the jacket, Ahlam calls for peace between Arabs and Jews, and proclaims their revolt against reason to be a "non-violent Intifada." An exciting and accessible album even for Westerners who can't understand the words.

Mahmoud Ahmed: Ere Mela Mela

Hannibal/Carthage

This Ethiopian recording dates from the mid-seventies, making it a forerunner of the style later known as rai. Ahmed's gruff and smokey voice mixes with bluesy sax and complex cross-rhythms you've come to expect in popular African music, but here it's mixed with Eastern harmonies, giving you a sweet taste of both worlds.

Annabouboula: Greek Fire

Cassette $9.80; CD $14.80 ppd (NJ residents add sales tax) from: Shanachie Records, 37 E. Clinton St., Newton, NJ 07860; 201-579-7763

Dance club and party tunes done Greek-style; Anna Paidoussi's vocals float above both the sequencers and the mandolin-like *dubeks*. The dance rhythms are a nice contrast to the minor-key Eastern melodies, adding a dynamic tension that most dance records lack.

Asia Classics 1: Dance Raja Dance

Luaka Bop/Reprise

Vijaya Anand is the modern magpie of Indian film music, copping sounds from American and Latin pop and updating Hindi movie soundtracks, a major source of Indian pop. In Vijaya's tunes, melodies can mutate from a country & western melody into a strange crossbreed of Samba and Punjabi dance, then on into disco.

Amazonia:
Cult Music of Northern Brazil

Cassette $12.98 ppd from: Lyrichord Discs Inc., 141 Perry Street, New York, NY 10014; 212-929-8234

The centuries-old collision of African slave, Indian and Portuguese culture in Brazil has produced a unique musical language inextricably tied to dance and religion. The Candomblé sect of the Yoruba religion developed a series of master patterns and cross-rhythms that evolved in popular form into the samba, the best known Brazilian pop musical style. This recording is a psychic excavation into the roots of that Brazilian music.

The bulk of the album is taken up by visits to Batuque cult houses in and around the north Brazilian town of Belém. Spirits are invoked; believers are possessed. In the background of one track, recorded at a festival for the Yoruba deity Ogum, you can hear fireworks and rockets going off as the dancers and players celebrate the arrival of one of their most important gods.

Music like this always sounds strange to non-native ears at first. It's an account of people who believe in a direct experience of god, ecstasy and the supernatural. It has little to do with the comparatively dry and removed religious experience of Christian society. That's one of the reasons European missionaries tried to wipe out these old gods and worked so hard to convert these people. Basically, the locals scared the shit out of the Europeans. The qualitative difference between, say, the ritual of eating the host and of having god herself descend on you, possess your body and ride you like a crack-crazed Appaloosa though the swamp, is burned into every moment of this recording.

Sheila Chandra:
Weaving My Ancestors' Voices

Real World

Those familiar with Chandra's densely orchestrated pop albums might be surprised by this largely *a cappella* recording. It's a personal exploration of the singer's voice, moving from traditional Indian "beat singing" (where a vocalist speaks the beats usually played by the tabla), to raga styles, to ballads from Ireland and Spain.

A surprising and personal album of one woman's world of music.

Also recommended: The Struggle; Silk; Third Eye; Compilasian

Dissidenten: Life at the Pyramids

Cassette $9.80; CD $14.80 ppd (NJ residents add sales tax) from: Shanachie Records, 37 E. Clinton St., Newton, NJ 07860; 201-579-7763

Less slick than their recent releases, these rootsy earlier recordings put less emphasis on the European synth-pop sound and are closer to what you'd likely hear in a Tangier dance club.

Also recommended: Sahara Elektrik

Exotica: The Best of Martin Denny

Cassette $11.98; CD $15.98 ppd (CA residents add sales tax) from: Rhino Records, 2225 Colorado Ave., Santa Monica, CA 90404-3555

Before there was world music, there was Martin Denny. In Hawaii in the mid-fifties Denny started blending odd Eastern percussion (as well as the sound of his band doing bird calls!) into his infectious blend of laid-back swing and, well, exotica. There's something hokey yet weirdly compelling about Denny's sound. Imagine Peter Gabriel's band backing up Don Ho.

Peter Gabriel: Passion

Geffen

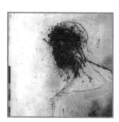

The soundtrack to the movie *The Last Temptation of Christ* uses elements of many traditional Middle Eastern musical styles, occasionally throwing in some Western twists and variations. If you're looking for a Peter Gabriel album, this will disappoint you as he is almost invisible, submerged in the larger sound of the music. But if you want a great album—and a good primer in the Mid-East feel and sound—this is the place to go.

George Mgrdichian Ensemble: One Man's Passion

Cassette $9.80; CD $14.80 ppd (NJ residents add sales tax) from: Shanachie Records, 37 E. Clinton St., Newton, NJ 07860; 201-579-7763

Egyptian dance melodies given a slightly jazzy Western treatment by *oud*-virtuoso George Mgrdichian and company. Traditional Eastern instruments are joined by electric bass, guitar and saxophone to create a flowing, energetic music that remains Eastern, but is transformed to something new and exciting by the deft introduction of jazz ideas. This isn't the "fusion" beast you often hear these days—a bunch of Western players pretending to be Eastern, playing Western music while clod-hopping around in a few Eastern modes. These are master Eastern musicians expanding the musical language of their remarkable native tongue.

Golden Voices from the Silver Screen, Vols. 1-3

Information from: Round World Records, 491A Guerrero, San Francisco, CA 94110; 415-255-8411

You will have one of two reactions to these discs—you will either love them and play them all the time, or they will drive you mad and make you want to tear all the skin off your face.

The three volumes of Golden Voices from the Silver Screen cover the music from "Movie Mahal," a British television history of the Indian film industry. Hindi film music tends to vary in mood from pure schmaltz to less pure schmaltz. The instrumental passages have a surprisingly familiar feel. It's the high-pitched, nasal female vocals that are the most interesting, and most foreign sound. There is no way around them; the singing is almost constant. You will love the vocals, grow to love them, or fall on the floor coughing up blood.

The Guo Brothers & Shung Tian: Yuan

Real World

A combination of folk and popular tunes from China. The songs evoke everything from bustling village streets, to ancient court

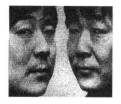

scenes, to a mad horse ride across the Mongolian plains. Like many Real World recordings this is a cross-cultural work, with a mostly Chinese band produced, and occasionally joined by, Irish songwriter and musician Pól Brennan.

Also recommended: Trisan

Jon Hassell: City

Opal/Warner

Hassell was playing world music decades before there was such a term. Vernal Equinox is a reissue of a 1978 LP, while City features more recent material. Vernal Equinox moves from ambient music to almost a funk groove at times, often hitting both extremes at once, with Hassell's breathy trumpet floating through dense waves of African and South American percussion. The vocal quality of Hassell's trumpet playing often gives an Arabic feel to his music; his sound is like the muzzein calling Muslims to prayer.

While Vernal Equinox is all jungle greens and mist, City glows like the business end of a laser scalpel. A tense blend of computer-driven drums, synths and Hassell's distinctive trumpet creates a sort-of be-bop tour of the world's great cities. If Miles Davis had starred in TRON, this would have been the soundtrack.

Also recommended: Dream Theory in Malay; Fourth World Volume 1: Possible Musics

Ofra Haza: Fifty Gates of Wisdom

Cassette $9.80; CD $14.80 ppd (NJ residents add sales tax) from: Shanachie Records, 37 E. Clinton St., Newton, NJ 07860; 201-579-7763

Haza's breakthrough album in the West, before she was swept off into Major Label Land, where her sound has become more and more diluted by Western pop cliches. Here, her sound is clean and dance-able, yet close enough to her Yemenite roots that you can still hear the desert sands shift in the background on her first international hit, "Galbi."

The Hugo Masters, Vols. 1 - 4

$18.48 ppd (CA residents add sales tax) from: Backroads, 417 Tamal Plaza, Corte Madera, CA 94925; 800-825-4848

Traditional Chinese musics, separated by type. Volume One covers "bowed strings." The *hu-chi'in*, Chinese bowed lutes, have a haunting, voice-like quality that mirrors the sinuous Chinese vocal style. Volume 2 features "plucked strings;" the main instrument here is the *P' i- p' a* (or *pipa*). Its sound has been imitated in a thousand bad movies, making it a more familiar sound. Volumes Three and Four cover wind instruments (different flutes and the *souna*, an adaptation of the Indian trumpet) and the wide variety of Chinese percussion. The well-written liner notes make this series an excellent introduction to a country with a long and rich musical tradition.

Nusrat Fateh Ali Khan: Devotional & Love Songs

Real World

You haven't heard singing until you have heard Qawwali, Sufi praise singing. Nothing is held back is these songs extolling the greatness of god. There is nothing like Qawwali in Western culture. It is the sound of joy, of religious rapture.

Nusrat Fateh Ali Khan performs with over a dozen members of his troop of family singers. At times the sheer force of all those voices is overwhelming.

Also recommended: Qawwal and Party Shahen-Shah; The Day, the Night, the Dawn, the Dusk

Shoukicki Kina and Champloose: Music Power from Okinawa

£16.99 air mail ppd (please pay with int'l money order) from: The Far Side, Marukin Biru 501, Yoyasu-machi 380, Kumamoto-Shi, Kumamoto-ken, T 860, Japan; fax 81-96-353-3615

A genuinely odd album for Western ears. Shoukicki Kina plays the *sanshin*, a 3-stringed plucked Chinese instrument that sounds oddly like a banjo. That sound combined with his loping rhythm section, and the sing-song melodies of his tunes ends up sounding like a mutant version of American country music. Recorded live, the loose feel of the disc makes an album that could have been a novelty item an odd pleasure.

Fela Kuti & Egypt 80: ODOO

Cassette $9.80; CD $14.80 ppd (NJ residents add sales tax) from: Shanachie Records, 37 E. Clinton St., Newton, NJ 07860; 201-579-7763

When black slaves were brought to America, the songs they brought with them mutated over time into many the rich varieties of music we now call American music—jazz, gospel, blues, etc. The sounds continued to evolve and when James Brown entered the scene, he brought with him a raging horn section and a heavy beat that was called funk. Eventually, these funk recordings made their way back to Africa where the rhythms were incorporated back into many of the local styles. The foremost funk-mesiter of Nigeria is Fela Kuti. He mixed Brown's funk with his own highlife-jazz and came up with a relentless weave of rhythm, horns, organ and voices, with many tunes lasting lasting more than 30 minutes. Hot and hypnotic, it's dance music with many political messages, but dance music nonetheless.

Also recommended: **Zombie**; **Beast of No Nation**; **Everything Scatter**; Teacher Don't Teach Me No Nonsense

Le Monde du Rai

$19.50 ppd from: Musicrama, 164 Driggs Ave., Brooklyn, NY 11222; fax 718-383-5152

This French CD may be the best single introduction to rai music available. Le Monde du Rai showcases a wide variety of Algerian pop, from the almost tribal opening number from Cheikha Remitti, to the youthful and more polished sounds of Cheb Mami and Cheb Kader. Because it's an import, Le Monde du Rai is expensive, but well worth the price. (The Muiscrama catalog lists the disc by its English name, The World of Rai.)

Tabu Ley: Babeti Soukous

Real World

In the West, Zairean rumba music is called soukous. With its upfront electric guitars and vocals, its relentless beat and big band format, it's one of the most popular styles to emerge from Africa. This album, recorded in the Real World studios, captures Ley's band performing in their natural element—live in front of an appreciative (if small) audience. The tracks are a mix of old and new styles, spanning Ley's 20 years as a leader in Zairean pop.

Lights in a Fat City: Somewhere

Information from: City of Tribes, 63 Fountain St., San Francisco, CA 94114; 415-469-2055

A stunning recording from England, combining the Australian didjeridoo with ancient percussion instruments from around the world, (throwing in the occasional found vocal for good measure). But it's the untraditional sound of the instruments that is fascinating here. Rather than going the obvious world music route, Lights in a Fat City has subtly processed their ancient instruments, giving them a shimmering modern feel. The pulse is restless and relentless. These are people playing; no sequencer could could touch this. A fascinating and original disc.

Lyrichord World Music Sampler

$13 ppd from: Lyrichord Discs Inc., 141 Perry Street, New York, NY 10014; 212-929-8234

A collection of traditional musics from around the world—Bolivia, China, Zimbabwe, Egypt, Tibet, Japan, Iran, Korea, and on and on... Greg Sandberg, the album's compiler, has put together an album of very disparate music that flows beautifully from one piece, one country, one style to another, forming a whole greater than its parts. An excellent introduction to traditional sounds from around the world.

Cheb Mami: Prince of Rai

Cassette $9.80; CD $14.80 ppd (NJ residents add sales tax) from: Shanachie Records, 37 E. Clinton St., Newton, NJ 07860; 201-579-7763

Dramatic, soaring vocals and driving rhythms characterize this urban pop expression of Arabic folk music. These are songs of love and passion filled with funky basslines and a dramatic call-and-response between Mami's strong voice and the sinuous violin.

The Master Musicians of Jajouka (Featuring Bachir Attar)

Axiom/Island

Straight from Morocco, the sound of pure ecstasy. The musicians of Jajouka are a caste unto themselves, generations of desert pop stars who make their double-reed horns sing, their drums moan. These are the sounds that drive dervishes into divine frenzies, seduce sheepherders, bandits and gods alike.

Stephen Micus: Wings Over Water

ECM

German performer Stephen Micus has been quietly making his own personal version of world music for years. From the time he started incorporating foreign instruments into his music, he worked to express his own interest in the instrument as a sound source, not as a way to copycat (for instance) Arabic music. On Wings Over Water Micus mixes traditional European instruments, such as the Bavarian zither, with the Egyptian *ney* flute, the Indian *sarangi*, a Balinese reed flute called a *suling* and a battery of tuned flower pots. The sound evokes a place far away, but not any one place, the kind of magical place you reach when you don't really have a destination in mind.

Also recommended: Darkness and Light; Implosions; East of the Night; The Music of Stones

Music of Indonesia, Vol. 2: Indonesian Popular Music

Smithsonian Folkways

When most people try to name the five most populated countries in the world, Indonesia doesn't often spring to mind as the fifth; too bad, it's the right answer. With an enormous population spread over 3000 islands, the culture of Indonesia, while predominantly Muslim, is a blending of dozens of different societies. It's this mass of disparate groups that gives Indonesian music its vitality, creating dozens of regional styles of Indonesian classical (gamelan) and pop music. It also makes it impossible to look at Indonesian pop without considering the politics of the country. The two dominant pop styles on this disc are *kroncong* and *dangdut*. *Kroncong* is a style that goes back to 16th-century Portuguese traders, who left both their instruments and freed slaves in the islands. The style developed from an urban folk music to a basis for radical revolutionary songs. Now it's considered a little hokey and old fashioned, like when your grandfather gets his Trotskyite buddies to sing a drunken round of "The Internationale."

Dangdut, on the other hand, is a still vibrant style, based on Indian, Western and Middle Eastern musical styles. It's favored by the young and restless Muslim youth (often from the poorer classes) who consider themselves more more hip and Western in their outlook. This style, like *kroncong*, also contains elements of social protest. And while simple sentiments like the Indonesian equivalent of "the rich get richer and the poor get poorer" sound tame to our ears, in conservative Indonesia, they are not unlike the Sex Pistols' radical tunes.

Natraj: The Goat Also Gallops

Information from: Accurate Records, P.O. Box 390115, Cambridge, MA 02139

Every animal lover knows that purebreds are often insane and prone to unpleasant congenital ailments; it's the mongrels that have the real vitality. This rule is exemplified by Natraj, a band that plays sort of a mongrel world jazz—combining influences from North Indian classical, West African tradition, and American jazz. Phil Scarff shines on sax in "Ava De Se," a variation on a traditional Ghanaian tune, and the Indian-inspired "Dha Ra Dha Tin Na." The Bulgarian,

"Dobro Dosle," is an unearthly-sounding violin and soprano sax duet. And the whole band comes together on an inspired version of Ornette Coleman's "Lonely Woman."

This is one of those rare albums that delivers the punch that world music promised, but often doesn't deliver.

Passion—Sources

Real World

This is the music that inspired **Passion**, Peter Gabriel's soundtrack for the film *The Last Temptation of Christ*. A real grab bag of styles, and excellent examples of traditional musics from Iran, Morocco, Guinea, Pakistan, Turkey, Egypt and India. A fine place to start your musical explorations.

Rai Rebels

Virgin Records

Rai is an urban pop music that started in the clubs around the port town of Oran, Algeria. Like most port towns, Oran posses a mongrel culture, retaining a strong sense of its North African heritage, but gleaning bits of the other cultures that brush up against it. Consequently, rai is essentially a North African style with heavy seasonings of Spanish, French, Bedouin, Moroccan and black African music. This compilation gives you six joyful dance bands, rocking and swaying like a cobra in a tux. The sound quality here is exceptional.

The Sabri Brothers: Ya Habib

Real World

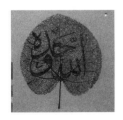

Qawwali, in a style similar to Nusrat Fateh Ali Khan, but the two Sabri Brothers perform on a much smaller scale, with the dominant accompaniment coming from harmonium and drums. A good complement to the Nusrat Fateh Ali Khan disc (see review on page 120), the Sabri Brothers give you a more intimate, though no less dynamic sampling of Sufi spirituals.

The Tahitian Choir: Rapa Iti

Triloka Records

The next time someone tells you that mass communication has ruined all our regional differences, pull out this disc. A 1,000 miles south of Tahiti is the dot of an island called Rapa Iti. For centuries the three hundred-something population has passed down its traditions and folklore in a haunting *a cappella* vocal style based on a quarter-tone scale system. French producer Pascal Nabet-Meyer went to the island and got the locals to perform their songs live in the village meeting place. The result is spontaneously joyful and compelling, a sound truly from another place and time. Another plus is that the album's liner notes translate most of the song lyrics, ancient creation stories and tales of war and discovery.

Ali Farka Toure: African Blues

Cassette $9.80; CD $14.80 ppd (NJ residents add sales tax) from: Shanachie Records, 37 E. Clinton St., Newton, NJ 07860; 201-579-7763

Not having been born into one of the traditional music clans of Mali, Ali Farka Toure had to sidestep centuries of custom and, sort of, invent his own musical style. What he came up with sounds uncannily like American Mississippi Blues. This album showcases both Toure's bluesy Malian guitar and warm, sonorous voice. The weird familiarity of Toure's style also makes this an excellent introduction to contemporary African acoustic music.

Trance Mission

Information from: City of Tribes, 63 Fountain St., San Francisco, CA 94114; 415-469-2055

Take Stephen Kent, the didgeridoo player from Lights in a Fat City (see review, page 122) and put him in a band with reed player Beth Custer, lots of percussion and some manipulated samples and you get something both exotic and alluring. This is the music that should have been behind all those big Hollywood exotica films—anything with a harem or a Mongol horde. Kent's droning didgeridoo, which can sound warm and earthy one moment, buzzing and electric the next, creates a firm foundation, over which the other

players can weave their sounds. The playing feels loose and sponta-
neous, spacious, like something you might encounter in some
dream desert in the middle of the night.

Also recommended: **Songs from the Burnt Earth: Didgeridoo Solos**

Voices

Mesa/Bluemoon

Occasionally a recording is so special, so overwhelming that it's hard
even to describe. Words like "amazing" and "spectacular" are so
cliched and lame, so I won't use them here, but simply say that if
you have any fondness for the sound of the human voice, then
Voices is something you must have. Simply, this is a three-CD set
with 33 cuts, 150 minutes, of some of the best choirs in the world.
Most of the globe is represented here, with singers from (for example) Tibet, Venezuela, Germany, Bali, Bulgaria, Japan, Germany,
South Africa and New Jersey. But be careful of a collection like this:
after repeated listenings, you will almost inevitably end up in the
record store, looking through the world music section for more
recordings by singers that have become permanently lodged in your
brain. Don't say I didn't warn you.

Yalla Hitlist Egypt

Mango

This is the Egyptian New Wave. **Yalla Hitlist Egypt's** 12 cuts cover
two current styles of Egyptian pop, *al jeel* and *shaabi*. *Al jeel* is the
sound of urban youth, a mixture of high-tech toys with ancient
Bedouin and Egyptian rhythms; sort-of an Egyptian dub consciousness, but with a disco drive. *Shaabi* is based on more traditional
Egyptian popular styles, tarted up for mainstream distribution, but
with the taste of sand and the call of the muzzein lurking in the
background all the time.

Psychotic Reactions and Carburetor Dung

by Lester Bangs; $15; Random House; 1987; 390 pp.

The *enfant terrible* of rock criticism set a new standard for sheer writing ability and intensity in the 70s. Here are memorable reviews and interviews, including takes on Lou Reed, Iggy Pop and The Clash.

Silence

by John Cage; $16.95; Wesleyan University Press; 1961; 276 pp.

Ironically, John Cage is probably better known as a writer than as a composer, because his music is played so infrequently, but his books have mostly remained in print. In Cage's first book, he ruminates poetically on listening, the structure of music, dance, composition, silence, mushrooms and Zen.

Africa O-Ye!

by Graeme Ewens; $27.95; Da Capo Press; 1992; 224 pp.

A fine introduction to the music of a very happening continent. Newer pop styles—rai, soukous, jit, etc.—are defined, explored and placed in the cultural context. Beautifully illustrated with both black & white and color photos.

Mystery Train

by Greil Marcus; $12.95; NAL/Dutton; 1975; 282 pp.

The best book about the emergence of an American pop culture; it traces the phenomenon by looking at the work and lives of Robert Johnson, Harmonica Frank, Randy Newman, The Band, Sly Stone and Elvis Presley.

Ancient Traditions—Future Possibilities

by Matthew Monfort; $27.45 ppd from: Ancient Future Music, P.O. Box 264, Kentfield, CA 94914-0264

Not just a book about world music, but a guide book on how to create it. Sections include styles of Northern and Southern India, West Africa and Balinese gamelan. In the "Future Possibilities" section, you see how to combine styles into something new, weird and beautiful.

Bring the Noise

by Havelock Nelson & Michael A. Gonzales; $12; Harmony Books; 1991; 298 pp.

Essential reference book on rap music traces the history of artists and producers as well as the culture that created them; lots of photos of performers, plus discography of must-have discs.

England's Dreaming (Anarchy, Sex Pistols, Punk Rock & Beyond)

by Jon Savage; $16.95; St. Martin's Press; 1992; 602 pp.

The history of the Sex Pistols' rise and fall becomes a treatise on the social conditions that produced the band and the general rise of anarchy in the U.K. Smart, but not out to prove how cool it is, this is the only essential book about the Brit punk scene.

New Sounds

by John Schaefer; OOP

I hate to mention an out-of-print book, but even though it's a bit dated on specific albums, **New Sounds** remains the best and smartest reference book on New Music. Haunt your local used book shops!

Robert Fripp (From King Crimson to Guitar Craft)

by Eric Tamm; $12.95; Faber and Faber; 1991; 242 pp.

An in-depth look at Fripp as musician, musical and social theorist and guitar icon. The last section in Fripp's Guitar Craft workshop is especially unsettling and revealing. Also recommended: **Brian Eno (His Music and the Vertical Color of Sound)**.

The Trouser Press Record Guide

edited by Ira A. Robbins; $18.95; Collier Books; 1991; 763 pp.

This new edition of **The Trouser Press Record Guide** contains reviews of around 9500 releases by 2500 (mostly) rock artists. What makes this book special is that the contributors went out of their way to include quality foreign (non-U.S.) and independent albums.

Incredibly Strange Music, Vol. 1

$21.99 ppd (CA residents add sales tax) from: RE/Search Publications, 20 Romolo, Ste. B, San Francisco, CA 94133

The folks who brought you **Incredibly Strange Films** now bring you this twisted guide to obscure vinyls, mostly from the 50s to the 70s. Hang out with the Cramps and their record collection. Learn about Jayne Mansfield's Shakespeare recordings, Jack Webb's love ballads, Godzilla sound effects discs and more!

1/1

$15/year (4 issues) from: Just Intonation Network, 535 Stevenson St., San Francisco, CA 94103

Quarterly journal of Just Intonation Network, promoting alternative tuning systems; subscription gets you network membership.

The Beat

$12/year (12 issues) from: Bongo Productions, P.O. Box 65856, Los Angeles, CA 90065

Reggae, Caribbean and world music, from Brazil to India.

Blues Access

$12/year (4 issues) from: Blues Access, 1514 North St., Boulder, CO 80304; fax 303-939-9729

The world of the blues, interviews, plus extensive reviews of recent releases and reissued discs.

Computer Music Journal

$38/year (4 issues) from: MIT Press Journals, 55 Hayward St., Cambridge, MA 02142-9902

Tech talk and theory on music, computers, MIDI and electronics.

Dirty Linen

$20/year (6 issues) from: Dirty Linen, P.O. Box 66600, Baltimore, MD 21239-6600

Folk, traditional and world music.

Eurock

$8/year (4 issues) from: Eurock, P.O. Box 13718, Portland, OR 97213

Electronic, progressive and avant-garde from around the world; short interviews, and extensive list of discs for sale.

Experimental Musical Instruments

$12/year (12 issues) from: Bongo Productions, P.O. Box 65856, Los Angeles, CA 90065

Design, construction and theories behind unusual instruments people make or invent themselves.

I/E

$16/year (4 issues) from: Think Tank Tomes, 2300 N. Yucca, Chandler, AZ 85224; fax 602-968-3619

Progressive and electronic music: Tangerine Dream, Djam Karet, PGR, etc.

IndustrialNation

$10/year (4 issues) from: IndustrialNation, 114-1/2 E. College St., #16, Iowa City, IA 52240

Industrial, techno, electronic, experimental; lots of interviews and reviews. Looks good, too.

Leonardo Music Journal

$35/issue ppd from: Pergamon Press, 395 Saw Mill River Rd., Elmsford, NY, 10523

Fairly technical annual concentrating on musicians who use technology in their work; comes with CD.

Negativland: The Letter U and the Numeral 2

$15.95 ppd (CA residents add sales tax) from: Silent Records, 540 Alabama St., #315, San Francisco, CA 94110; fax 415-864-7815

Negativland recounts the lawsuit brought against them by Island Records with first-hand documents and a CD.

Opal Information

$16/year (4 issues) from: Opal Information, P.O. Box 141, Leigh-on-Sea, Essex, England

Brian Eno's official information zine. Interviews, articles by and about Eno and his various projects.

Option

$16/year (6 issues) from: Option Subscriptions, 2345 Westwood Blvd., #2, Los Angeles, CA 90064

Best all-around zine of alternative music; each issue can hit folk, rap, rock, techno, avant-garde, world beat, etc.; lots of reviews.

Rejoice!

$10/year (6 issues) from: Rejoice!, Sam Hall, Room 206, University of Mississippi, University, MS 38677-9990

The world of gospel music; interviews, book and record reviews.

ReR Quarterly

£60/year (4 issues) from: ReR Megacorp, 19-23 St. Saviour's Rd., London SW2 5HP, England

Cerebral and visually lovely British zine concentrating on avant-garde music; your subscription includes CDs and printed material.

Society Pages

$20/year (5 issues) from: Society Pages, P.O. Box 395, Deer Park, NY 11729-0395

Zine of the International Frank Zappa Society; Frank's new projects, plus interviews with side men, such as Adrian Belew.

The Source

$19.95/year (12 issues) from: The Source, P.O. Box 586, Mt. Morris, IL 61054-7983

Hip-hop, rap, and the culture and politics that surround them.

Tellus

Cassette issues #7-24, $10 ppd each ($12 foreign); CD issues #25 & #26, $15.50 ppd each from: Tellus, 596 Broadway, #602, New York, NY 10012; 212-431-1130

Cassette (and now CD) zine highlights new and unusual audio arts. Recent *Tellus* issues include: audio works by visual artists, new music from China and women artists-in-residence at Harvestworks. Issues come with copious notes on performers and performances.

Africassette catalog free from: Africassette, P.O. Box 24941, Detroit, MI 48224; 313-881-4108

Cassettes straight from Africa, so you can hear artists such as Youssou N'Dour in their original non-watered down local versions. All cassettes are guaranteed; prices are around $12 per tape.

Anomalous Records catalog free from: Anomalous Records, 1044 N.E. Oneonta St., Portland, OR 97211-4074; fax 503-285-9689

U.S. and imported progressive, experimental and industrial CDs, tapes and LPs. An impressive roster of artists.

Asmara Compact Disc House catalog $3 from: Asmara Compact Disc House, 5568 Sepulveda Blvd., Culver City, CA 90230; fax 310-390-5250

Extensive collection of Indian recordings of all types, including regional styles such as Punjabi, Bengali, Tamil, etc.

Barking Pumpkin catalog $1.50 (and SASE) from: Barfko-Swill, P.O. Box 5418, N. Hollywood, CA 91616-5418

Frank Zappa's mail order record biz; for $1.50 you get the "Z/PAC"—Frank's catalog, plus his answer to music censors.

Bose Express Music catalog $10 from: Bose Express Music Catalog, The Mountain, Framingham, MA 01701-9323; 800-451-BOSE (outside U.S. 508-879-1916)

Excellent source of 75,000 mainstream record titles; the catalog is expensive, but comes with money saving coupons.

Cadence $25/year (12 issues) from: Cadence, Cadence Bldg., Redwood, NY 13679-9612; fax 315-287-2860

Interviews with jazz performers, and reviews of new albums; center of zine is a tiny-print-eye-strain catalog of recordings of all types of improvised music, from jazz to New Music.

Celestial Harmonies catalog free from: Celestial Harmonies, P.O. Box 30122, Tucson, AZ 85751

World music, electronic, jazz, modern classical, New Music; from the famous (Paul Horn, Phil Manzanera, Steve Roach, etc.) to the ought-to-be.

The Far Side catalog free from: The Far Side, Marukin Biru 501, Yoyasu-machi 380, Kumamoto-Shi, Kumamoto-ken, T 860, Japan; fax 81-96-353-3615

Large catalog of releases from all over the Far and Middle East: Japan, Hong Kong, Indonesia, Pakistan, Thailand, Turkey, Malaysia, etc.

Hatikvah Music International no catalog, call or write with requests: Hatikvah Music International, 436 N. Fairfax Ave., Los Angeles, CA 90036; 310-655-7083; fax 310-938-0577

Importer and distributor of recordings from all over the Middle East; especially strong on Israeli and archival Jewish recordings.

Heartbeats catalog free from: Backroads Distributors, 417 Tamal Plaza, Corte Madera, CA 94925; 800-825-4848

New age, space music, modern classical, New Music, self-help; some books and videos, too.

Ladd-Frith catalog free from: Ladd-Frith, P.O. Box 967, Eureka, CA 95502; fax 707-443-5366

Indy cassette and CD distributors and performers; sounds from ambient to rock to techno.

Ladyslipper catalog free from: Ladyslipper, P.O. Box 3130, Durham, NC 27705; 800-634-6044

Music by women from all over the world; some of these recordings appear in no other catalogs.

Lyrichord Discs catalog free from: Lyrichord Discs, 141 Perry St., New York, NY 10014; fax 212-929-8245

Traditional and modern recordings from all over the world; they have an excellent world music sampler CD for only $11.

Original Music catalog $1 from: Original Music Catalog, 418 Lasher Rd., Tivoli, NY 12583; fax 914-756-2027

Modern and traditional recordings of world music; impressive tapes from the Irish Folklore Commission and archival recordings of important African discs. Also have videos and books.

Rashid Sales Company catalog $1 from: Rashid Sales Company, 191 Atlantic Ave., Brooklyn, NY 11201; 800-843-9401

Number one importer of Arabic and Middle Eastern music of all kinds, from traditional to new rai releases.

Rhino Records audio catalog $3 from: Rhino Records, 2225 Colorado Ave., Santa Monica, CA 90404-3555

Contemporary indy artists and classics by the likes of Bonzo Dog Band, James Brown and Blue Cheer; also blues, soundtracks, comedy, spoken word and kids' recordings.

ROIR catalog free from: ROIR, 611 Broadway, # 411, New York, NY 10012; 212-477-0563; fax 212-505-9908

Cassette-only label specializing in dub, punk, industrial and electronics. Lots of out-of-print recordings and rare stuff from musicians' vaults.

Round World Records catalog $2 from: Round World Catalog, 491A Guerrero, San Francisco, CA 94110; 415-255-8411

CDs, tapes, LPs and videos from all over the world; very knowledgeable and helpful staff. Call if you can't find something.

Rounder Records catalog free from: Rounder Records, One Camp St., Cambridge, MA 02140

"Roots" and traditional musics: bluegrass, blues, Cajun/Zydeco, reggae, children's music and lots of small indy labels.

Shanachie Records newsletter free from: Shanachie Records, 37 E. Clinton St., Newton, NJ 07860; 201-579-7763

Reggae, Celtic, South American, blues, Afropop, etc. Also an impressive video collection.

Silent Records catalog free from: Silent Records, 540 Alabama St., # 315, San Francisco, CA 94110

Industrial, noise, techno, experimental and extreme recordings of all kinds; many imports. Also books, zines and videos.

Sound of Pig catalog $1 from: Sound of Pig, c/o Al Margolis, P.O. Box 150022, Van Brunt Station, Brooklyn, NY 11215

Indy cassettes: noise, progressive, experimental, industrial. The Cassette Conspiracy lives here.

Stern's Music catalog free from: Stern's Music U.S., 598 Broadway, 7th Fl., New York, NY 10012; fax 212-925-1689

The killer world music outlet in the U.S.; pop and dance from Africa, the Caribbean, South America, Europe, the Near, Middle and Far East, etc.

Sub Rosa catalog free from: Sub Rosa, 171 ave. du Diamant, 1030 Brussels, Belgium; 322-733-0905; fax 322-736-7974

New and progressive music from Europe and around the world. Their Made To Measure series is an outstanding introduction to new music, composers and performers. They'll ship orders virtually anywhere in the world.

Introduction—Video

Back when Hollywood was the alpha-male of the entertainment biz, it produced and released around 800 movies a year. That was decades ago, back before movies cost as much as a Stealth Bomber to make, and before toys like videocams and VCRs cost no more than a good 35mm still camera. Home video has permanently changed the landscape of visual entertainment.

Video has mutated into a generic term, referring to nothing more than a distribution medium. At any moment, all over the world, hundreds of small and medium-sized movies are being produced.

You won't get a chance to see most of these movies in your local theaters because of distribution and censorship battles, the cost of foreign translations, miniscule ad budgets and a general lack of information. But now you can find films that vanished from the theaters on video, films such as science fiction cult hit *Tetsuo* (page 145) and the politically disturbing *Through the Wire* (page 148).

There's also film-to-video's younger, nastier sibling—the direct-to-video release. Most of these films are junk—zero-forehead exploitation rip-offs with derivative car chases, unconvincing chainsaws and perky babes in pointless shower scenes. Others, such as *Beyond the Mind's Eye* (page 138) and *Hey Folks, It's Intermission Time!* (page 140), can permanently invert your neural net.

In addition to the videos reviewed, you'll also find sections on books and zines covering video and film topics such as Hong Kong cinema, black filmmakers, Italian thrillers, 60s sexploitation flicks, cheesy monster features and the whole range of extreme video dubbed "psychotronic." There's also a directory of video mail-order outfits that sell (and sometimes rent) all of the titles reviewed, plus lots more—enough addresses to make your mailbox a lot more exciting.

A note: anyone interested in videos from foreign sources should check out the Aiwa HV-M110 reviewed on page 202, in the Tools For Living section. The HV-M110 can play and/or record in all the major videocassette formats (PAL, MESECAM, NTSC 3.58 and NTSC 4.43).

Akira

$32.95 ppd (CA residents add sales tax) from: Streamline Pictures, P.O. Box 691418, W. Hollywood, CA 90069

This was (and might still be) the most expensive animated feature ever made in Japan. Combining elements of *Blade Runner*, juvenile delinquent B-movies and "the kid with special powers" scenario (a tradition in Japanese pulps) in a vivid post-post-holocaust setting, *Akira* is epic science fiction. The main story lines concern the motorcycle-riding Kaneda's search for his pal Tetsuo (who has been kidnapped by some government baddies who want to experiment on him), Tetsuo's emergence as a telekinetic superman and the answer to the question, "Just who was Akira?" There are scenes of violence, disturbing hallucinations and intrigues that boot *Akira* immediately out of the superhero cliches that drive a lot of Japanese animation, placing it on a whole new quality level. The art direction, cinematography and soundtrack are worthy of any big budget Hollywood production, and the final violent blow-out at the end of the film, with Kaneda trying to destroy the wildly mutating Tetsuo, is the type of insane over-the-top action that imaginative adventure films always promise, but seldom deliver. *Akira* delivers the goods, many times over.

Beyond The Mind's Eye

$23.45 ppd (WA residents add sales tax) from: Miramar, 200 Second Ave. West, Seattle, WA 98119; 800-245-6472

Like most video compilations, *Beyond The Mind's Eye* is a mixed bag of the beautiful and the banal, the familiar and the strange. *Beyond The Mind's Eye* isn't presented just as an assemblage of bitching high-gloss graphics, however. There's a hook. It's structured as a sort of trip through the human psyche. This isn't a new conceit, but works best when the images aren't too familiar. When certain commercial graphics pop up, for instance, it's hard not to think, "Hey look, it's those Hawaiian Punch robots!" Fortunately, most of the footage isn't too common. The best moments of animation from *Lawnmower Man* are here, as are some "scientific visualizations" and startlingly realistic nature animations. Some of the shots of hummingbirds, and a mid-air combat sequence between two bees (that includes a long tracking shot through a hollow log) are outstanding computer recreations of real objects.

The low point of the tape is Jan Hammer's obvious and under-whelming soundtrack music. If you like state-of-the-art computer animation, you'll like *Beyond The Mind's Eye*, but you'll probably want to turn down the sound.

Bizarre Rituals:
Dances Sacred and Profane

$79.95 ppd (CA residents add sales tax) from: Gauntlet Mail Order Service, 1201 Old County Rd., Unit 3, Belmont, CA 94002

From Mardi Gras, to New York S&M clubs, to an American Indian initiation ceremony, we follow photographer and teacher Charles Gatewood as he continues his explorations of "American subcultures." In this case, Gatewood is looking at body manipulators; along the way, he meets Fakir Musafar, a man whose own body manipulations started when he was a boy of 12. Much of the film concerns Gatewood's conversations with Musafar, as they talk about the spiritual side of body manipulation, and the historical drive to find transcendence through pain. The last section of the film follows Fakir's preparation and performance of the Sun Dance, an American Indian ritual in which the subject is suspended by steel hooks through his chest. After Gatewood meets Fakir, the film takes on the air of a quest, both for the photographer and his subject. A sympathetic and intelligent look at what Gatewood calls "Liberation through excess."

Because there is quite a bit of nudity in the film, you must state that you are over 21 when ordering this video.

Fakir Musafar is pierced by the "Spears of Shiva" in an Indian Kavandi-bearing ceremony.

Common Threads

$25 ppd (CA residents add sales tax) from: The NAMES Project, c/o Merchandise Coordinator, 2362 Market St., San Francisco, CA 94114; 800-USA-NAME

This Academy Award-winning film is the story of five lives—a gay Olympic athlete, an eleven-year-old hemophiliac, an IV drug user, a successful landscape architect, a nurse—and an idea. After all five people contracted AIDS, their lives became part of the idea: the AIDS Memorial Quilt. The quilt, which began as a movement among friends in the Bay Area has become a national symbol of the lives that are the reality behind the terrible statistics of AIDS deaths. The five quilt panels represented by the people covered in *Common Threads* are now part of a display that covers over 14 acres. *Common Threads* documents both the lives and deaths of five people, and the beginning of the Memorial Quilt project, ending with the dramatic Washington, D.C. quilt display.

Common Threads is narrated by Dustin Hoffman, and features music by Bobby McFerrin. All profits from the film go to the NAMES Project to keep displaying and caring for the AIDS Memorial Quilt.

Hey Folks, It's Intermission Time!

$23 ppd (WA residents add sales tax; make checks payable to Mike Vraney) from: Something Weird Video, Dept. F.U.N., P.O. Box 33664, Seattle, WA 98155; 206-361-3759, 10 a.m. to 10 p.m.

This tape must be the video equivalent of collecting snowglobes or little spoons with the names of the states on them—an inexplicable obsession. *Hey Folks, It's Intermission Time!* is almost two hours of drive-in intermission reels—you know, the films they showed between features with dancing hotdogs and jumbo Cokes? This tape goes further, however, by collecting regional reels, including ads for local barbecue joints and lumber yards. There's even a little period politics thrown in with attacks on the newly threatening medium of TV, and a 50s vintage plea for patrons to write their newspapers to "stop daylight savings time!"

Fanny Fatale shows you where to put your speculum (and why) in *How to Female Ejaculate*

How to Female Ejaculate

$42.95 ppd (CA residents add sales tax) from: Fatale Video, 526 Castro St., San Francisco, CA 94114; 800-845-4617

Sex professional Fanny Fatale, the star of *How to Female Ejaculate*, describes sexuality as a source of power. She advocates that women increase their knowledge of the G-spot and female ejaculation as a route to a more integrated sex life. Besides, as the video makes clear, learning more about sex can be a whole lot of fun.

The video is divided into three parts. The first third is rather clinical: Fanny describes the anatomy of the vagina and the G-spot. In the second section, three other women join Fanny for a frank discussion about orgasms, masturbation, and ejaculation. The discussion segues into the final section, a sexual slumber party in which the women take out their sex toys, demonstrate their masturbation techniques, and ejaculate on camera. Throughout the tape, the women are refreshingly down to earth. My favorite comments included "Where'd you get that hot pink dildo?" and "I always use rubbers on my dildos. It keeps them clean." Finally, the video includes recommended reading for further research. A very practical approach to increasing sexual awareness and pleasure. —Mary Maxwell

The Mahabarata

$105.95 ppd from: Parabola, P.O. Box 2284, S. Burlington, VT 05407; 800-843-0048

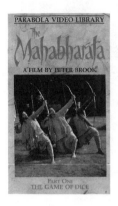

The Mahabarata is Peter Brooks' nine-hour stage-play-into-film interpretation of India's national epic. Unlike the 3-hour cut that hit U.S. theaters last year, this is the full-length uncompromised version of the work.

A story of feuding families, secret deals between humans and the gods, wars and desire, the film presentation retains much of its original stage feel, with stylized movements and speech. Despite this, or perhaps because of it, the film works very well. By using a wandering narrator, stylized acting and theatrical sets that are neither outside nor quite inside, Brooks successfully heightens the alien, mythic quality of the work.

No Such Thing As Gravity

$25 ppd from: Atomique Film, 110-20 71st Road, Forest Hills, NY 11375; 718-520-0354

Let's face it—low-budget science fiction is usually the bottom of the barrel, where cheap effects, bad acting and dumb ideas can leave you feeling like your brain just got a toxic waste wax job. But like a lot of trash culture, when the right person comes along, the whole idea can be revived. The Hernandez Brothers did it for comics with **Love and Rockets**, and director Alyce Wittenstein might do it for SF-on-the-cheap with *No Such Thing As Gravity*.

The film is both an homage to and a satire of all those lame SF movies you grew up watching late at night when you were supposed to be in bed. While this might have been enough to be amusing, Wittenstein takes it further, making the cheapness of the out-of-context sets into something weirdly beautiful. She also gets more out of her actors than those 50s potboilers ever did, charging her movie with a nervous energy and sexiness that would have sent Hugh Beaumont and John Agar screaming for the hills.

You don't need to know the plot, because if you grew up watching black & white SF, you already know the plot. If you love SF, then get *No Such Thing As Gravity*, and if you hate SF get it anyway; it just might make you a believer.

Also recommended is stylish video-of-manners and homage to Godard, *Betaville*.

The Pleasures of Uninhibited Excess

$28 ppd ($33 foreign; CA residents add sales tax) from: Survival Research Laboratories, 1458-C San Bruno Ave., San Francisco, CA 94110

Mark Pauline and Survival Research Laboratories have been around for more than ten years, staging startling and violent performance events in which their gruesome homemade machines are unleashed on stage sets and each other. The machines are the only players in SRL's shows, walking, crawling, rolling and occasionally flying across the performance area like mechanized Bosch demons. The themes of SRL's shows are almost always political, the staging blackly comic in its over-the-top combination of crashing metal, ear-blistering noise and flames.

The Pleasures of Uninhibited Excess documents both three spectacular SRL performances, and as a bonus, the version available straight from SRL (as opposed to the Warner Brothers version) includes hysterical TV coverage of the mysterious appearance all over the Bay Area of scary looking objects marked "Explosives"....

Peril or Pleasure

$35 ppd ($45 foreign) from: Torrice Productions, 1230 Market St., #123, San Francisco, CA 94103

This video explores a recent debate among feminists: Is there such as thing as feminist pornography? Can performing in or producing sexually explicit films and magazines be an act of liberation in which women take control of their sexuality, making conscious choices as to how best use their minds and bodies, or is all pornography destructive, objectifying women, and playing into men's worst stereotypes?

Peril or Pleasure presents compelling spokeswomen for both sides. At one extreme, Evelina Kane of Women Against Pornography states that pornography, "is the most prevalent form of sex education in this country." This, Kane maintains, distorts the self-image of teenagers and adults alike. At the other end of the spectrum, Candida Royale, an ex-porn star and head of Femme Productions, a woman-oriented adult film company, says about porn, "What I'm going to do is take it into my own hands, do it the way I think it should be done, and have control over it. That to me is a very feminist thing." Also featured in the film are adult film director/producer Annie Sprinkle and San Francisco's own sex diva, Susie Bright.

Peril or Pleasure doesn't come to any definitive answers on the pornography/feminism debate, but it's one of the best and clearest presentations of the arguments yet. This documentary is an important contribution to the ongoing debate over women's rights and issues of sexual freedom.

Suburban Dykes

$37.95 ppd (CA residents add sales tax) from: Fatale Video, 526 Castro St., San Francisco, CA 94114; 800-845-4617

I have a theory: erotic videos made by women for women always feature excellent underwear. But *Suburban Dykes*, starring Nina Hartley, Pepper, and Sharon Mitchell, has much more than sexy lingerie. Here's the story: A couple of cute dykes (Nina and Pepper) decide to spice up their sex life. The spice includes voyeurism, a phone call to a dominatrix line, and a visit from a lesbian escort service (Sharon).

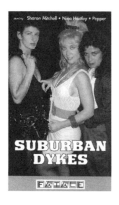

It's hot, it's fun, and it inspired me to become a card-carrying member of the Sharon Mitchell fan club. And you can even defend it as politically correct. Since 1984, Fatale Video has been producing erotic lesbian videos, part of a movement of women who are creating woman-oriented erotic material. An announcement at the start of the video declares: "These materials reflect the feminist right for control over our bodies, thereby promoting female sexual autonomy." Assert your feminism, admire some great lingerie, and have a good time. Who could ask for more? —Mary Maxwell

Director Shinya Tsukamoto appears as the title character in his film, *Tetsuo*

Tetsuo: The Iron Man

$83.90 ppd from: Fox Lorber Video, 419 Park Ave. S., New York, NY 10016; 800-862-8900

A surreal and funny action film that's sort of a cyberpunk retelling of Kafka's "The Metamorphosis." Only in this version we get to see the transformation from briefcase-toting Salaryman to monster (an amorphous combination of flesh and metal). Combining a driving industrial soundtrack with amphetamine-laced pacing, an undercurrent of violent eroticism and threads of black humor worthy of Lynch or Buñuel, director Shinya Tsukamoto pulls off something Hollywood finds almost impossible: creating a film that's both accessible and capable of showing you things you've never seen before.

Scientific Visualizations

Scientific Visualizations Volume One, & Mandelbrot Sets and Julia Sets, $24 each ppd (CA residents add sales tax) from: Media Magic, P.O. Box 598, Nicasio, CA 94946; 800-882-8284; Retinaburn, $17.95 ppd (CA residents add sales tax) from: Ray Vonne Filmworks, 1118 Capello Way, Ojai, CA 93023; 805-640-1732

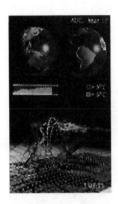

Ever seen computer animations of, for instance, changes in the Earth's temperature over the next 100 years, or the vibrating insides of a molecule? Did you ever wonder where those animations come from? They were probably generated using computer models at the National Center for Supercomputer Applications. Now on two videos, you can see some of the best highest-tech computer animations in the world.

Scientific Visualizations Volume One contains computer-generated storms, greenhouse effects, fires in Yellowstone, a black hole spacetime demo and dancing hydrogen atoms.

Mandelbrot Sets and Julia Sets is two full hours of super-computer generated fractal imagery. Graphically, a fractal is a shape whose overall shape is repeated indefinitely. Some of the dozens of fractal studies on this tape use the super-computer's drawing power to "zoom" into a small section of the fractal. In a few minutes, you realize that you are looking at exactly the same shape you started from. For anyone who missed psychedelics in the 60s, this tape will not only give you a hint about what everyone else was looking at, but the booklet accompanying the tape will explain exactly what all those bifurcated lines mean. It's accompanied by two hours of original electronic music.

In a lighter, but related vein is *Retinaburn*, a silent fractals video. It's graphically more dynamic and sexy than *Mandelbrot Sets and Julia Sets*. The idea on *Retinaburn* is that you provide your own music and setting, maybe your living room with Led Zeppelin, or a rave with blistering techno.

"Harry Smith worked on these movies secretly, like an alchemist, and he worked out his own formulas and mixtures to produce these fantastic images."
—*The Village Voice*

Harry Smith:
Heaven and Earth Magic

$34.90 ppd from: Mystic Fire Video, P.O. Box 2249, Livonia, MI 48150; 800-292-9001

The phrase "Yankee ingenuity" stood for the cleverness that seemed to arise spontaneously in American society where anybody with an idea could follow it to its ends, and have the idea judged solely on its merits. From the early 40s through the early 60s, Harry Smith created a number of extraordinary animated films. Part of what makes the films special is what makes Watts Towers and things like bluegrass music special; these are folk arts created and performed by the unschooled artists who invented them. Harry Smith's mysterious and dreamlike animations are both art of the highest order and spiritual journeys. *Heaven and Earth Magic* tells a surreal and funny parable through animated Victorian collages, while its companion tape, *Early Abstractions*, creates rich images using nothing more than color, light and movement. The films of Harry Smith share a vision as intense and personal as any magician's spellbook or any artist's palette.

VIDEOS . . . .

Through the Wire

$83.90 ppd from: Fox Lorber Video, 419 Park Ave. S., New York, NY 10016; 800-862-8900

In 1986, three women—self-described "political prisoners"—were transferred to a secret underground isolation unit in the Federal Prison in Lexington, Kentucky. The unit later became infamous in the human rights community and became known as "the first political prison in the United States." In the constantly lit prison, the women were subjected to sleep deprivation, round-the-clock surveillance, daily strip and body cavity searches and constant video monitoring including, during the early months, while they showered. During the course of the film, the women age visibly. None of the women, however, renounced their political affiliations.

Through the Wire is the story of both the women and the special prison-within-a-prison in which they spent two terrible years. The film is also a cautionary tale, showing you how basic human rights can vanish in an instant, even in supposedly "free" countries.

Towers Open Fire

$34.90 ppd from: Mystic Fire Video, P.O. Box 2249, Livonia, MI 48150; 800-292-9001

William Burroughs is not only an innovative author, but he worked with friends like Anthony Balch and Brion Gysin in film experiments during the early 1960s. Many of these experiments are gathered together in Mystic Fire Video's *Towers Open Fire*. Burroughs' use of language and imagery, especially in combination, is designed to break down your existing thought processes, and let you see the control mechanisms that want to run your life.

A related title, *William Burroughs: Commissioner of Sewers*, is a fine complement to *Towers Open Fire*. It's a series of interviews and readings, wherein Burroughs lays out his basic philosophy of life and work.

Trailers

Trailers on Tape, $38.45 each ppd from: Trailers on Tape, 1576 Fell Street, Suite #1, San Francisco, CA 94117; 415-921-8273; Martial Arts Mayhem, $21.45 ppd from: BOOPzilla Productions, 54 Turner Street #3, Brighton, MA 02135

One of the best parts about going to the movies is seeing the trailers for upcoming releases. At their best, trailers are micro-movies in themselves, distilling the 100 minutes of a feature into two or three minutes. Often, the trailer for a movie is better than the movie itself.

Trailers on Tape is an outfit that has collected dozens of old trailers (between 60 and 75 minutes' worth per tape) onto 16 videos including musicals and adventure movies, Alfred Hitchcock, science fiction and horror. Two of Trailers on Tape's funniest and sleaziest titles are *Psychotronic: Midnight Movie Madness* (everything from *The Texas Chainsaw Massacre* to *Citizen Kane*), and *AIP: Fast and Furious* (American International's exploitation flicks like *Wild in the Streets* and *Beach Blanket Bingo*). Write to them for their complete catalog.

Martial Arts Mayhem is a collection of two dozen Chinese, Japanese and American martial arts film trailers, including promos for films by Bruce Lee, Chuck Norris and Jackie Chan. The picture quality is excellent, although there are a few technical problems (the picture isn't always centered, etc.), but they're minor and frankly, for these movies, kind of make it more fun. Sort of like going to that broken down drive-in out by the interstate.

Leatherface from *The Texas Chainsaw Massacre*

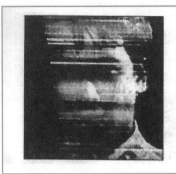

THEY BEGIN
PRODUCTION
OF HUMAN
DUPLICATES
—"DUPES"—
TO FURTHER
THEIR ENDS
ABOVE
GROUND.

Tribulation 99:
Alien Anomalies Under America

$19.99 ppd; book $6.66 ppd; both for $25 from: Craig Baldwin, 992 Valencia St., San Francisco, CA 94110

For hardcore conspiracy buffs, *JFK* was a mere bauble. For the pure product conspiracy rant of your lifetime, try *Tribulation 99*. Told in a fast-paced, Apocalyptic jump-cut style, *Tribulation 99* uses stentorian oratory and stolen B-movie footage to rip the lid off the conspiracy of evil extraterrestrial Q-men who manipulate world events from their lair in the center of the Earth. Their goal? To destroy the human race! See the evil Qs assassinate President Kennedy! See their human duplicates cover up weird cattle mutilations! See them bug Democratic Party headquarters in the Watergate Hotel!

Filmmaker Craig Baldwin has blended together historical fact with the paranoia of dozens of rants and crank theories lifted from books and tracts into perhaps the ultimate video paranoia-fest. As if that wasn't enough, Baldwin has produced a handsome book based on the film, full of the same images and narration. Beware! This, too, could be part of the conspiracy!

Also recommended is Baldwin's revisionist "discovery of America" video, *O No Coronado!*

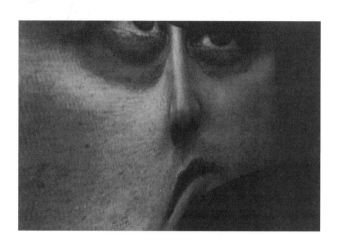

WAX or the Discovery of Television Among the Bees

$36 ppd from: David Blair, Box 174, Cooper Station, New York, NY 10276

Combining archival footage with new video, David Blair gives us the extraordinary feature, *WAX*. As densely layered as any novel, *WAX* is a tale of transcendence. It tells the story of computer programmer and beekeeper Jacob Maker and the discoveries he makes when he hears the voices of the bees in his hives and learns that the bees are the link between this world and the land of the dead. But that's only a small part of the multi-generational, multi-dimensional story of *WAX*. Moving between his own past and his future, Maker travels to the land of the dead, and to Iraq during the Gulf War, ending his time on earth as a smart bomb zeroing in on an Iraqi tank.

The force of Blair's vision is evident in every frame of *WAX*. Both the writing and visuals of *WAX* are superb. Working on a low budget, he made an end run around ordinary special effects, and used simple computer-generated images to create startling and memorable visions of both the bees' world view and the land of the dead.

It's not often that a film or video comes out of nowhere, kicks down the door and demands to be seen. *WAX* is the exception that proves the rule—a low-budget independent video feature that works on many levels, and heads off in directions most video and film makers wouldn't go near.

From Bruce Lee To The Ninjas: Martial Arts Movies

by Ric Meyers, Amy Harlib, Bill and Karen Palmer

Citadel Press; 1985; 255 pp.
$18.85 ppd from: Jars Video Collectibles, Attn: Joseph Ragus Sr., P.O. Box 113, Little Neck, NY 11363; 718-456-0663

This is the best, and maybe the only, intro to martial arts movies. It includes chapters on Chinese and Japanese history, *chambara* (Japanese swordfight) films, stars and directors like Bruce Lee, Jackie Chan, Chang Cheh, Liu Chia Liang, and many others, along with lists of the ten best and worst martial arts movies, actors' aliases, martial arts techniques and lots of photos. It's sloppily organized and, most annoyingly, lacks an index, but it's an immensely useful book all the same. The Palmers (both jiujitsu black belts) are reportedly working on a sequel.

Asian Trash Cinema

$20/year (4 issues; $10/issue #1) from: Craig Ledbetter, P.O. Box 5367, Kingwood, TX 77325

ATC is "the bastard step-child of *European Trash Cinema*" (see review, page 166), Craig Ledbetter's other movie zine. Like its step-dad, *ATC* concentrates on the seamy side of movies—stuff like Malaysian "mondo shockumentaries," and Thai slasher movies—but covers the whole spectrum of Asian action cinema, avoiding the traditional chop socky stuff. A slick, digest-sized, color-covered zine, *ATC* is determined to cover every base. Definitely order a back issue of #1, which contains about 400 reviews—an essential guide through this vast territory.

Martial Arts Movie Associates

$10/year (4 issues) from: William Connolly, 6635 De Longpre #4, Hollywood, CA 90028

Ric Meyers and the Palmers (see previous review) teamed up with Bill Connolly to produce *M.A.M.A*; it's "a clearing house for all the

gossip we hear, all the movies we see, and all the videos we view." And they see everything. They also have some great connections in the Hong Kong film biz, and regularly provide insider gossip and interviews with stars and directors. This is the least fancy zine of the bunch—typewritten and anything but pretty—but more than makes up for it in scope of knowledge.

Oriental Cinema

$6/issue from: Damon Foster, P.O. Box 576, Fremont, CA 94537-0576

What can you say about Damon Foster's zine? Well, it's an ambitious, personal, one-man labor of love—40-50 jam-packed pages of reviews, articles and photos of Asian action movies written, edited and designed by Foster himself. It looks great, and Foster's obviously a committed collector, but he's also very, very cranky. His reviews often begin with, for instance, an account of his trip to see the movie —including all the details of his encounters with ex-girlfriends, bad Chinese food and people less cool than him. If you don't mind wading through all of his odd asides, it's quite a piece of work.

Jars Video Collectibles

Catalog $4 from: Jars Video Collectibles, P.O. Box 113, Little Neck, NY 11363; 718-456-0663 (call from 7:30 a.m. to 10:30 p.m. only)

They can fill all your Hong Kong video needs via mail-order, from old kung fu chop sockies to the latest John Woo hail-of-bullets special. Fast, reliable and reasonably priced (most videos go for $20.00 to $40.00). When you order a video, you automatically receive the Jars newsletter, and catalog updates.

Video Search of Miami

Catalog free from: Video Search of Miami, P.O. Box 16-1917, Miami, FL 33166; 305-279-9773

Another great HK video mail order source. They also carry lots of other hard-to-find exploitation-type stuff from all over the world.

Laurie Anderson: Home of the Brave

$22.98 ppd (AZ and PA residents add sales tax) from: Spectrum Music Video, P.O. Box 1128, Norristown, PA 19404; 800-846-8742

Laurie Anderson is an artist and a conceptualist as much as a musician. Her elaborate stage shows have become the stuff of legends, combining performance, video, computer graphics, masks, monologs and—yes, even music.

Anderson herself directed this concert video of her *Sharkey's Day* tour. Backed by an amazing band that includes Adrian Belew on guitar and David Van Tieghem on percussion, and with a special appearance by William Burroughs, the concert is as inspiring, funny, sexy, hummable and memorable as any show you're likely to see.

Also available is a compilation of Anderson's videos and shorts, simply called *Laurie Anderson: Collected Videos*. The tape includes Anderson's original "O Superman" video, and Laurie introducing and hanging out with her rather unlikely looking (male) clone.

Chet Baker: Let's Get Lost

$22.98 ppd (AZ and PA residents add sales tax) from: Spectrum Music Video, P.O. Box 1128, Norristown, PA 19404; 800-846-8742

Perhaps you've seen pictures of the defoliated jungle in Vietnam—places of dead earth and withered tree trunks that look like the sad result of some terrible natural disaster, only the devastation is too precise to be anything but manmade. The first glimpse of be-bop trumpter and vocalist Chet Baker's face in *Let's Get Lost* is like seeing that corrupted landscape, something that was once beautiful and alive, that has been beaten raw and savaged by chemicals

This profoundly melancholy film is as much about Baker's face as it is about his music; it's that face that charts his Pilgrim's Progress from the 50s, when he was the trumpet-playing James Dean-good-looking hipster, to the ravaged husk of a man in the 80s, wasted by years of alcohol and junk. But even at that late stage, Baker's music has its power, and it holds together this biographical film. In the end, *Let's Get Lost* is as restless, driven and compelling as the man whose life it portrays.

Beats of the Heart

Information free from: Shanachie Records, 37 E. Clinton St., Newton, NJ 07860; 201-579-7763

Beats of the Heart is an exciting video series from Shanachie looking at ethnic music from all over the world, including Tex-Mex, Zydeco, Afro-Cuban, Township Jive, Reggae and Gypsy music. A couple of outstanding titles include *There'll Always Be Stars In The Sky*, an inside look at the Indian film industry (a major source of pop music in India) and *Rhythm of Resistance*, an overview of South African pop when apartheid was still the rule of the land. Each tape is 60 minutes, and goes for about $20, so it's hard to go wrong.

Paul Dresher: Slow Fire

$28 ppd from: Minmax Music, 235 Surrey St., San Francisco, CA 94131

Not a music video at all, but a document of Dresher and Rinde Eckert's performance piece. Dresher's minimalist music score sprints along, a soundtrack of dread and ecstasy. Eckert is riveting as he sings, recites and shouts a text of American images and platitudes, some beautiful, many banal. There is an undercurrent of suppressed violence in the performance. By the end of the piece, Eckert's neutral white jumpsuit has been replaced by shades and a business suit cut from camouflage material.

Emergency Broadcast Network: Commercial Entertainment Product

$19.98 ppd (AZ and PA residents add sales tax) from: Spectrum Music Video, P.O. Box 1128, Norristown, PA 19404; 800-846-8742

Techno beats sliced and diced with media sights and sounds. No one and no thing is spared. The video and audio samples range from George Bush to Jimi Hendrix, Bill Clinton to Mr. Rogers, Dan Rather to Bud Dwyer. It all gets cuisinarted together into glistening kidney punch agitprop, Situationist Busby Berkeley numbers that go after drug and gun hysteria, two-faced politicos and the media itself.

Brian Eno: Imaginary Landscapes

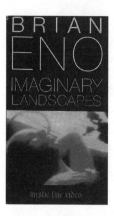

$29.90 ppd from: Mystic Fire Video, P.O. Box 2249, Livonia, MI 48150; 800-292-9001

Imaginary Landscapes is part documentary, part peek inside the head of the artist, as familiar Eno tunes are placed against his homemade videos, combining abstract images with shots of New York, the U.S. southwest, the interior of science museums, Hollywood and Venice. The pace is leisurely, but compelling; it doesn't demand your attention, it simply gathers your attention into itself, much like Eno's music.

Eno's other major video, *Thursday Afternoon*, presents a series of tableaus that change slowly over time. The images are a visual analog of Eno's ambient music—a part of the total environment.

Philip Glass: Koyaanisqatsi

Rental only $10/night (from time you sign with UPS until return package is postmarked) from: Crystal Mountain Music Video, P.O. Box 1299, Glenwood Springs, CO 81602; 800-433-8574

The ultimate music video. 90 minutes of non-stop images (natural and manmade structures) and music. The word *Koyaanisqatsi* is Hopi for "life out of balance." Although the video is a cautionary tale of life lived in excess, filled with images juxtaposing (for instance) the Grand Canyon with south Bronx tenements, it is also beautiful and, ultimately, uplifting. When the images and Glass's score mesh, it's just like flying.

Gwar: Tour de Scum

$22.98 ppd (AZ and PA residents add sales tax) from: Spectrum Music Video, P.O. Box 1128, Norristown, PA 19404; 800-846-8742

What can you say about Gwar? They are by turns the worst and best metal band on the planet. Their stage shows are works of putrid art, and often, just putrid. If you've never seen them, imagine Josie and the Pussycats set in a Flintstones universe, but all of the members of the band are possessed alternately by Jerry Lewis and Satan. Don't bother with the albums. For Gwar, stick to the videos.

Matt Heckert:
Mechanical Sound Orchestra

$15.50 ppd from: We Never Sleep, Box 92, Denver CO 80201

Heckert is an alumnus of Mark Pauline's Survival Research Laboratories robot performance group. Heckert applies some of SRL's overpowered hydraulic tendencies to machines that, primarily, don't blow up, but make noise/sound/music in interesting ways. This video explores the sounds and the processes behind these machines. Hieronymus Bosch meets Rube Goldberg and jams with Luigi Russolo.

Henry Kaiser: Eclectic Electric

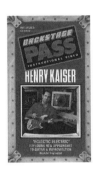

$52.95 ppd (AZ and PA residents add sales tax) from: Spectrum Music Video, P.O. Box 1128, Norristown, PA 19404; 800-846-8742

While this is, technically, a music instruction video, don't let that stop you from checking it out. Henry Kaiser sounds like no other guitarist around, and in between explanation of his effects set-up, and his theories of who and what music to listen to, he plays a lot of wonderful tunes with the likes of Jin Hi Kim and John French. It's this eclectic grouping of musicians that says more than words about the breadth of Kaiser's talent.

Master/Slave Relationship:
Forced Abandon

Information from: Master/Slave Relationship, P.O. Box 191211, San Francisco, CA 94119-1211

Like her CDs and tapes, Debbie Jaffe's Master/Slave Relationship video confronts questions of gender, sex, power, eroticism, pain and violence. The simplicity and obviously low-budget production standards of the videos on this tape make them even more compelling, like perverse home movies. Master/Slave Relationship's power is both to arouse and to disturb, and Jaffe does both on this compilation. You must be over 21 to order.

David Lynch/Angelo Badalamenti: Industrial Symphony #1

$22.98 ppd (AZ and PA residents add sales tax) from: Spectrum Music Video, P.O. Box 1128, Norristown, PA 19404; 800-846-8742

Nowhere is David Lynch's dark romantic vision more fully expressed than in the stage presentation, *Industrial Symphony 1 (The Dream of the Broken-Hearted)*. Fortunately, Lynch captured his own stage work on video for everybody who missed the original.

Lynch's perennial chanteuse, Julee Cruise, in prom queen white, literally floats above a set full of ravaged images of American romanticism: a 50s car, a rural electrical tower, a hint of a junkyard in the background—these are dream images of innocence, the open road, the end of the line. As Cruise sings songs by Lynch and Angelo Badalamenti, a man in a tuxedo (another prom night refugee?) searches in vain for the love he lost. A woman appears on the electrical tower, half dancing, half writhing. Is this who the man is looking for? Hints of jealousy, paranoia, violence—even war—saturate the background. The juxtaposition of Lynch's devastated images against Badalamenti's lush music is both touching and sinister.

The Residents: 20 Twisted Questions

Laserdisc $52.95 ppd (postage is approximate and varies on your location; CA residents add sales tax) from: The Voyager Co., 1351 Pacific Coast Highway, Santa Monica, CA 90401; 800-446-2001; Video Voodoo, $32.95 ppd (AZ and PA residents add sales tax) from: Spectrum Music Video, P.O. Box 1128, Norristown, PA 19404; 800-846-8742

Technically not a video, but a laser disc compilation of twenty years worth of The Residents' films, videos, computer animations and performances. Some of the early pieces on this disc, such as "Hello Skinny" and "The Third Reich and Roll," make clever use of simple collage effects, staging and lighting to turn the minimal productions into a part of the piece. Included are some recent computer animations from their *Freak Show* album (and upcoming CD-ROM), and performance footage from their extraordinary "Cube-E" show.

If you don't have a laser disc player, you can see many of the pieces from this disc on the tape *Video Voodoo*.

The Arc Group

Catalog free from: The Arc Group, P.O. Box 410685, San Francisco, CA
94141-0685; 800-727-0009

Distributors of a number of New Age, "visual music" and nature-ori-
ented videos. In *Earth Dreaming*, Steve Roach's ambient synthesizer
music is set to graceful shots of the southwest U.S. in which photographer Georgianne Cowan finds many natural analogs of the female
form. In *Structures from Silence*, Marriane Dolan uses Roach's music as
a background for an animated Voyager-like tour though space.
Watercolors is more visually and aurally kinetic. It contains Denise
Gallant's short video pieces that range from purely abstract forms to a
virtual-winter setting to a solarized seascape, all set to a pleasant
rhythmic score.

Crystal Mountain Music Video

Catalog $5 from: Crystal Mountain Music Video, P.O. Box 1299,
Glenwood Springs, CO 81602; 800-433-8574

A wide range of music videos, plus they have some non-music videos,
too, including exercise and foreign language instruction. They also
rent movies.

Spectrum Music Video

Catalog $2 from: Spectrum Music Video, P.O. Box 1128, Norristown,
PA 19404; 800-846-8742

My favorite music video catalog. Calling the Spectrum Music Video
catalog exhaustive is kind of like saying the Hoover Dam uses a bunch
of concrete. Their videos include rock, jazz, easy listening, country,
New Age, gospel and more.

Step Right Up!

I'm Gonna Scare the Pants Off America
by William Castle
$12.95; Pharos Books
1992; 264 pp.

The king of exploitation films, William Castle, had a career that spanned five decades. In various capacities, he worked with Bela Lugosi, Orson Welles, Roman Polanski and Marcel Marceau. But he's best loved for his horror films of the 50s and 60s and for his methods of promoting them. Probably his most famous gimmick was for *The Tingler*; Castle had theater seats rigged with motors "...to buzz the asses of everyone in America...." The projectionist would press a button whenever the Tingler appeared on screen and the audience would jump.

This autobiography is a wonderful tour through Hollywood from the 40s to the 70s. Besides the exploitation films, Castle details his work on scores of other films, from *The Lady from Shanghai* to *Rosemary's Baby*. His frightening story of the making of the latter film is alone worth the price of the book. There's a reverent introduction by John Waters. —Mark Faigenbaum

Men, Women and Chainsaws

(Gender in the Modern Horror Film)
by Carol J. Clover
$12; Princeton University Press
1992; 260 pp.

Men, Women and Chainsaws is a thoughtful feminist look at modern horror films, though it probably isn't at all what you expect it to be. There are no knee-jerk attacks on filmic violence or horror here; author Carol J. Clover looks beyond what's on the surface of the screen to dig out the meaning and power of such films as *The Texas Chainsaw Massacre* and *I Spit On Your Grave*. The latter film, a brutal rape and revenge tale, is one that Clover looks at closely.

At the heart of Clover's thesis is the idea that what makes horror films interesting (and powerful) is that they permit viewers not only to switch points of view (from victimizer to victim), but that they're one of the few places where viewers of both sexes can come into direct contact with a female (as the classic horror victim) point of view. And since horror is a pop culture artifact, this cross-gender identification comes with little of the distancing found in most high art. Using examples such as *Ms. 45* and *Carrie*, Clover points out that while some critics are disturbed by audiences that respond enthusiastically to the brutality in many horror films (like the rape in *I Spit On Your Grave*), the same audiences will cheer even louder when the female character acts out her violent revenge on her attackers, switching allegiances to traditional power roles and sex roles, too.

Whether you agree with Clover's conclusions or not, reading **Men, Women and Chainsaws** will have you reconsidering whatever cozy ideas you have, not only about horror films, but about any media presentation of horrific or violent images. And in an age when riots and wars are carried live on TV, that can't be a bad thing.

A Youth in Babylon

Confessions of a Trash-Film King
by David F. Friedman with Don De Nevi

$19.95; Prometheus Books
1990; 355 pp.

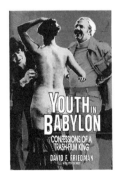

Hungry to catch a glimpse of the forbidden, from the 40s to the 60s, Americans flocked by the millions to drive-ins, road shows and movie houses to see the latest exploitation movies. Lured by lurid ads and the promise of being shown it all, the audience usually got far less than it thought it was going to get.

David F. Friedman hawked, huckstered and conned these movies into any venue he could get. He booked fake hygiene films (i.e., full frontal nudity films) for the grandfather of exploitation, Kroger Babb, and later, working with Herschell Gordon Lewis, produced some of the earliest 60s nudie films and the first splatter film, *Blood Feast*.

Packed with stories of his time on the road with the kings of exploitation, **A Youth in Babylon** takes us to backwater drive-ins, Christian censorship boards, courtrooms and dingy strip joints as Friedman spins tales of life in the low-budget and often low-talent world of exploitation films. Keep your eyes peeled for volume two of Friedman's story. —Mark Faigenbaum

Nightmare of Ecstasy

The Life and Art of Edward D. Wood, Jr.
by Rudolph Grey
$14.95; Feral House
1992; 231 pp.

Edward D. Wood Jr., was a man driven to create, and the films that he created in the 50s, 60s and 70s will be here for us to enjoy as long as there's a video store with a well-developed sense of bad taste. A transvestite with a divine lust for angora sweaters and an ex-marine, Wood wrote, produced and directed such grade-Z classics as *Plan 9 from Outer Space* and *Glen or Glenda*.

Wood's story is told through interviews with his friends and associates, his stars and his widow. It is a very funny and ultimately tragic story of a Hollywood dream. Wood died a destitute alcoholic at the age of 54. Also included is a comprehensive chronology, filmography and a listing of all his known exploitation novels and short stories. Recommended for Wood fans and those just curious about that strange world down in southern California. —Mark Faigenbaum

The Bare Facts

by Craig Hosoda
1993; 620 pp.
$13.95 ppd (CA residents add sales tax) from: The Bare Facts, Box 3255, Santa Clara, CA 95055-3255; 408-249-2021

If they gave college degrees in voyeurism, Craig Hosoda would qualify for a doctorate. In this Third Edition of The Bare Facts, Hosoda and his crew catalog nude scenes by 1,600 actresses and 650 actors in hundreds of movies. But that's not all. Almost all of the scenes in the book are from films available on video, and every instance of nudity is noted with the duration (for example, Ann Magnuson in *The Hunger*: "0:05—Brief topless in kitchen with David Bowie before he kills her"); star ratings let you know just how hot the scene gets. The Bare Facts is a good example of how intensity can turn an essentially silly idea into something amazing.

Incredibly Strange Films

1986; 220 pp.
$17.99 ppd (CA residents add sales tax) from: Re/Search, 20 Romolo St., Ste. B, San Francisco, CA 94133

A connoisseur's guide to *outré* film and video. The book opens with a series of interviews with such trash luminaries as Herschell Gordon Lewis, Russ Meyer, Frank Henenlotter and David Friedman. Other essays look at specific film genres, such as biker and J.D. flicks, women in prison, educational and "industrial jeopardy" films. It's also indexed.

The X-Rated Videotape Guide 3

by Robert H. Rimmer

$18.95; Prometheus Books
1993; 242 pp.

Rimmer's supplement to his previous porn film reference works, **The X-Rated Videotape Guide, volumes 1** and **2**. Volume 1 reviews adult films made from 1970 to 1985; Volume 2 looks at porn produced from 1986 to 1991; Volume 3 covers 1990 to 1993, and indexes all three books.

Cronenberg on Cronenberg

edited by Chris Rodley

$19.95; Faber and Faber
1992; 197 pp.

Through in-depth interviews that range in topic from his early experimental films to theories of biology and philosophy, David Cronenberg explains his whole career. Many interesting stories and facts emerge—such as how Sue Helen Petrie, the star of *They Came From Within*, begged Cronenberg to slap her silly just before filming when she realized she couldn't generate her own tears. The book covers all of Cronenberg's work, including his commercials, TV work and the little-known racing film *Fast Company*, through his acting role in Clive Barker's *Nightbreed*, and his most elaborate directing gig, *Naked Lunch*.

The Samurai Film

by Alain Silver
$12.95; Overlook Press
1983; 242 pp.

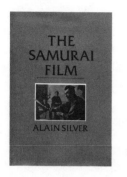

An excellent introduction to a genre of films as rich, varied and insightful about Japanese society as westerns are about America. Silver puts the samurai in the context of Japanese culture before getting into film specifics; he draws on his extensive film knowledge not only to look at the history of samurai film, but to show how it relates to and has influenced other films, comparing, for instance, the end of Kurosawa's *Seven Samurai* with Sam Peckinpah's *The Wild Bunch*. **The Samurai Film** is illustrated with fine still photos.

Shock Value

by John Waters
$14.95; Delta
1981; 243 pp.

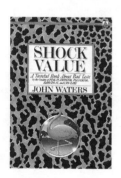

Unlike many filmmakers, John Waters is no stranger to the written word. In fact, even if you hate his films, he's such a good writer that there's a better than even chance that you'll like his books. **Shock Value** is subtitled "A Tasteful Book about Bad Taste," and easily lives up to its claim. In these thirteen essays, reports and reminiscences, Waters talks about why he makes his films the way he does, his unique casting methods, his fetish for attending trials (he got into both the Patty Hearst and Manson trials), and answers such burning questions as why he still lives in Baltimore, "Why I Love Violence" and "Do You Have Parents?" What emerges is a portrait of a smart and funny guy who had the energy, talent and balls to reinvent himself as a successful filmmaker, one who still thrives on controversy.

Psychotronic Encyclopedia of Film

by Michael Weldon
$20; Ballantine Books
1983; 815 pp.

The editor of *Psychotronic Video* (see review, page 169) has concocted

a reference book with reviews and credits for more than 3,000 of the cheapest, craziest and most appalling movies ever made. Starting with *Abbott and Costello Go to Mars* and ending with William Castle's *Zotz!*, Weldon hits almost every type of trash cinema you can think of, from sexploitation to caveman films to beach movies to Grade-Z science fiction. This is a hilarious and essential book for any film fanatic. And volume two is in the works!

Hardcore

by Linda Williams

$12.95; University of California Press
1989; 330 pp.

In the introduction to **Hardcore**, Linda Williams confesses that she originally thought that writing about hardcore pornography was going to be a toss-off job, a single chapter of a larger book, a chapter "that would require no new thought or research." Her background in feminist studies and politics had her prepared to see the subject in a canned combination of Freud and feminist critique of porn as the total objectification of the female body and the dominance of the phallus. When she studied a large number of hardcore films, however, she found that her original assumptions had been wrong.

Williams found something much more anxious and ambiguous in pornography, "a remarkable uncertainty and instability." She goes on to say that, "I began to see that an understanding of how power and pleasure function in discourses in which women's bodies are the object of knowledge could be crucial to any efforts to alter the dominance of male power and pleasure in the culture at large...." **Hardcore** is the result of her studies. In it she offers not only a serious (and balanced) look at the aesthetics of pornography, but attempts to "get beyond the question of whether pornography should exist to a consideration of what pornography is...."

Script City

Catalog $2 from: Script City, 8033 Sunset Blvd., #1500, Hollywood, CA 90046; 213-871-0707

An excellent source of 8,000 original scripts for feature films and TV episodes and movies; they also carry film books, photos and posters.

Adam Film World
Directory of Adult Films

$11.45 ppd ($13.45 foreign; CA residents add sales tax) from: Film World Directory 1993, Dept AFW, 8060 Melrose Ave., Los Angeles, CA 90046-7082

Annual zine with reviews and stills from more than 1,000 mainstream porn films. Also contains star profiles, source directories and indexes by theme, title and moviemaker. The same company also produces an annual *Directory of Gay Adult Video* for the same price.

Adult Video News

$48/year (12 issues; $150 foreign; CA and PA residents add sales tax) to: AVN Publications, 8600 W. Chester Pike, #300, Upper Darby, PA 19082; 215-789-2085

The ins and outs (so to speak) of the adult film and video biz. Lots of ads, gossip and reviews of mainstream adult, amateur and gay videos. This really is a news zine; don't get it if you want titillation.

Black Film Review

$12/year (4 issues; $22 foreign) to: Black Film Review, P.O. Box 18665, Washington, D.C. 20036

Blacks in film as actors, directors and producers. This is a nicely put together zine is co-produced by the Black Film Institute and the University of the District of Columbia. It also looks at TV and video, and contains reviews, calendars of events and filmographies.

European Trash Cinema

$20/year (4 issues) to: Craig Ledbetter, P.O. Box 5367, Kingwood, TX 77325

Sister zine to *Asian Trash Cinema* (see review, page 152). *European Trash Cinema* explores European exploitation genres, such as Italian *giallo*, or thrillers. Issues usually contain interviews with directors, nude starlets and lots of often interesting, sometimes hostile, letters.

Fatal Visions

$6/issue ($24/6 issues in Australia only) from: Fatal Visions, c/o Michael Helms, P.O. Box 133, Northcote, VIC, 3070, Australia

An Australian look at trash cinema and exploitation films. Looks at films and video from Russ Meyer, to Hong Kong crime and fantasy epics, to director Peter Jackson's career in bad taste comedy/horror films. Lots of reviews and interviews.

Film Threat

$12/year (6 issues; $22 foreign) from: Film Threat, Subscriptions Dept., P.O. Box 16928, N. Hollywood, CA 91615-9960

A slick, professional-looking zine devoted to over-the-edge and independent films, where attitude is half the game. They also take great joy in punching enormous holes in the Hollywood establishment's sense of self-importance by, for instance, running lists like their annual Frigid 50—the show biz figures who've had enough bombs to see their careers go cryogenic.

Film Threat Video Guide

$24.95/4 issues (includes free video) from: Film Threat Video Guide, Subs. Dept., P.O. Box 3170, Los Angeles, CA 90078-3170

The nasty little brother of *Film Threat* concentrates on the independent video scene and market, profiling filmmakers whose work is mostly known to a video audience; it also catalogs dozens of independent vids, from the deservedly obscure to gems such as *Nekromantik* and *Tribulation 99.*

Highball

$6.95/issue from: Kronos Publications, MPO Box 67, Oberlin, OH 44074-0067

Slick zine looking at sexploitation films—mostly softcore films that were thought of as porn before porn was readily available. The first issue has interviews with R. Lee Frost and Barry Mahon, as well as articles on Bardot, grindhouse flicks and sex films from Germany that portrayed themselves as "medical reports."

Imaginator

$6/issue (£2.20 U.K.; $4.50 Europe) from: Imaginator, c/o Ken Miller, Unit 1, Hawk House, Peregrine Park, Gomm Road, High Wycombe, Buckinghamshire, HP13 7DL, U.K.

A zine heavy on interviews with exploitation film actors and directors. Interviews in one issue: Ray Harryhausen, Patty Mullen (star of *Frankenhooker*), Mark Houghton (Hong Kong bad guy), martial artists Cynthia Rothrock and Jerry Poteet and *Orgy of the Dead* director, Steve Apostolof. Video, film and zine reviews.

Laser Disc Newsletter

$35/12 issues ($50 foreign) from: Laser Disc Newsletter, P.O. Box 420, East Rockaway, NY 11518-0420

Reviews and news from the laser disc biz. Alternate releases are sometimes reviewed together (often video vs. laserdisc, but sometimes, alternate laser releases, too). Not a pretty zine, but stuffed full of good info. If you're into laser discs, this is a "must have" item.

LaserScene Monthly

$25/year from: LaserScene Monthly, c/o Scott A. Hughes, 37 Dorland St., San Francisco, CA 94110

Reviews of current foreign and domestic laser disc releases. Also reviews of remastered discs and features looking at related releases, such as film noir on laser disc. Each title is rated on content and disc quality. Also includes lists of unreviewed discs released that month.

Monster International

$3.50/issue from: Kronos Publications, MPO Box 67, Oberlin, OH 44074-0067

From the folks who bring you *Highball* comes a monster movie zine. Issue two contains an exhaustive look at Mexican horror, the erotic horror of Jesus Franco, Italian Guns, Gator and Gore features, plus features and reviews of rare and notorious cinema, such as *The Golem* and *Entrails of a Virgin*.

Psychotronic Video

$20/6 issues ($22 Canada; $45 foreign airmail; $50 Asia, Australia & New Zealand) from: Psychotronic Video, 3309 Route 97, Narrowsburg, NY 12764-6126; fax 914-252-3905

Psychotronic Video is wall-to-wall data on the sleaziest, cheapest and most unforgettably bad movies on tape. In one issue: a complete David Carradine filmography and interview, a primer on Brazilian horror movies, a peek at the career of the *Creature from the Black Lagoon's* squeeze Julie Adams, a look at Boris Karloff's last decade making cheap Mexican horror flicks, loads of hard-to-read video reviews, star obituaries, plus obsessively crammed ads.

Video Watchdog

$24/year (6 issues; $33 foreign) from: Video Watchdog, P.O. Box 5283, Cincinnati, OH 45205-0283; 513-471-8989

One of the best (or worst) kept secrets in the film/video world is that many films exist in different versions; some changes are simply cosmetic, such as retitling. In some cases, changes can be dramatic— including scenes added or dropped or alternate dialogue; this is especially true now that rival versions of films can appear on TV, video and laser disc. And let's not even mention different European and Asian releases. *Video Watchdog's* whole reason for existence is to track these different versions, and report back to its readers on the best and worst available. For video collectors, this zine is essential. The editors recently gathered a combo of old and new material into the excellent **The Video Watchdog Book** ($20 ppd; $25 foreign).

We Are the Weird

$19.95/26 issues ($35/52 issues; $70 foreign) from: We Are the Weird, P.O. Box 2002, Dallas, TX 75221

Joe Bob Briggs' weekly newsletter of American culture and drive-in trash cinema. Joe Bob, in case you don't know, is sort of a redneck Calvin Trillin, and his reviews meander from bizarre personal anecdotes to the number of breasts, decapitations and car crashes in each movie. He's politically incorrect and often very funny.

Absolute Beta, 105 E. Washington St., P.O. Box 130, Remington, VA 22734; 800-937-2382; catalog free; membership $9.95

A video club with hundreds of old and recent releases on Beta. Membership gets you bimonthly updates and newsletters, video searches and membership discounts.

AnimEigo, P.O. Box 989, Wilmington, NC 28402; 919-251-1850; Fax 919-763-2376; catalog free

Huge selection of quality Japanimation, including the *Bubblegum Crisis* series, *Vampire Princess Miyu* and *Madox-01*, a parody of all those "armored suit" cartoons.

Beta Library, P.O. Box 836224, Promenade Station, Richardson, TX 75083-6224; catalog free

Beta format videos, from artsy films such as Antonioni's *Zabriske Point* to goofy Al Yankovic music videos. New customer specials give you discounts toward future tapes with each tape you buy.

Discount Video Tapes, 833 "A" N. Hollywood Way, P.O. Box 7122, Burbank, CA 91510; 818-843-3366; fax 818-843-3821; catalog free

100s of tapes, all priced from $20 to $40. They also rent tapes by mail.

Fatale Video, 526 Castro St., San Francisco, CA 94114; 800-845-4617

Producers of erotic videos by and for lesbians. Recommended tapes are *Suburban Dykes* and *Bathroom Sluts*, the latter a hot example of lesbian amateur sex videos.

Femme Distribution, 588 Broadway, #1110, New York, NY 10012; 212-226-9330; catalog free

Ex-porn star Candida Royalle's video company produces hot and classy erotic tapes oriented toward couples. But don't think these are wimpy—Royalle has some of the big names working for her; women like Nina Hartley, Sharon Kane, Taija Rae and Siobhan Hunter.

Flash Publications, P.O. Box 410052, San Francisco, CA 94141; catalog free

Charles Gatewood's documentaries look at extreme subcultures—tattooists, piercers and fetishists of all kinds. And his travel vids are like none you've seen.

Four Play Video, 10314 Norris Ave., Ste. G, Pacoima, CA 91331; 818-715-0008; 800-662-7529; catalog free

The *Dirty Debutantes* amateur video series features some of the best and worst in sex tapes. The worst is the usual assortment of leering studs doing come shots. But *Dirty Debutantes* also features people acting out taboo fantasies and liking them; it's one of the few places in sex vids where you'll see people smiling and laughing.

Media Magic, P.O. Box 598, Nicasio, CA 94946; 415-662-2426; catalog free

Science education videos: Computer animations, scientific visualizations, fractals, medical imaging, chaos theory, general science, astronomy.

Mystic Fire Video, P.O. Box 2249, Livonia, MI 48150; 800/292-9001; catalog free

A fabulous range of titles covering the old and the new, feature films and documentaries: Joseph Campbell's *Power of Myth* series, Derek Jarman's films, William Burroughs and Lydia Lunch performances, the Indonesian documentary *Ring of Fire* and Kenneth Anger's short films. And lots more!

Neighborhood Girls, P.O. Box 191544, San Francisco, CA 94119; catalog free

Amateur sex vids featuring ordinary people, either solo women or couples. You must be 21 or older to order.

Over The Top Video, P.O. Box 12733, Raleigh, NC 27605-2733; catalog $3

Russ Meyer's entire sexploitation film catalog on video in one place! These are the legit releases, and not lame third-generation bootlegs.

Rhino Home Video, 2225 Colorado Ave., Santa Monica, CA 90404-3555; 800-843-3670; catalog free

Vintage music videos, kidvids, old TV, offbeat horror, and great 50s and 60s exploitation titles, some gathered in double feature packages such as *Saturday Night Sleazies*—a whole evening's entertainment in a box!

The Right Stuf, P.O. Box 71309, Des Moines, IA 50325-1309; 800-338-6827

Great animation from Japanese TV—*Astroboy*, *Gigantor*, *The Eighth Man*, etc. Plus T-shirts, posters and books.

Sinister Cinema, P.O. Box 4369, Medford, OR 97501-0168; 503-773-6860; catalog free

Horror, suspense, science fiction and serials on video, all for about $17 a tape!

Something Weird Video, Dept. F.U.N., P.O. Box 33664, Seattle, WA 98155; 206-361-3759; catalog $2

Comprehensive catalog of softcore sexploitation films dated from the 30s through the early 70s, including Betty Page bondage flicks. Also carry B horror.

Whole Toon Catalog, P.O. Box 369, Issaquah, WA 98027-0369; 206-391-8747; fax 206-391-9064; catalog free

Cartoons! Featuring intense Japanese adventure toons, *Flintstones*, *Ren & Stimpy*, Disney, etc. Cartoon-related toys, and some laserdiscs, too.

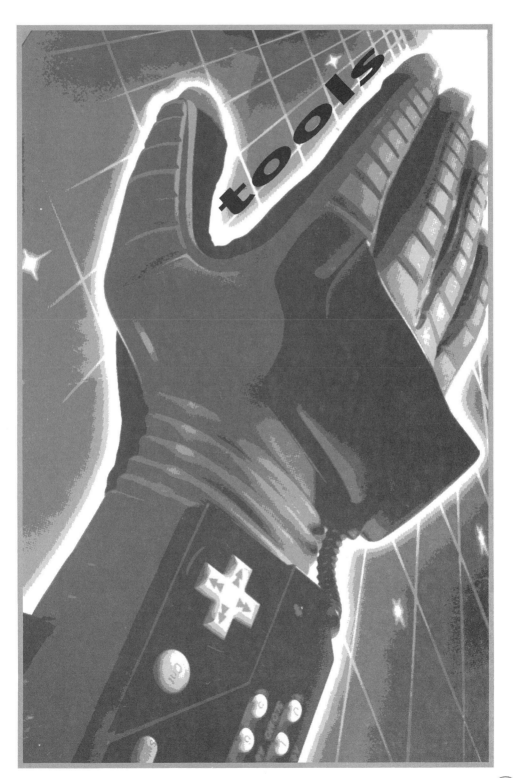

tools

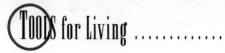

Introduction—Tools for Living

I used to work in a warehouse where the boss had an interesting perspective on tools. According to his worldview, anything that couldn't be fixed with a broom or duct tape was too far gone to matter. He would deep six the item, whether it was a cracked window or a forklift.

What is a tool? There are probably as many tools as there are desires and obsessions. I'm not talking about the kind of tools you need to cherry-out an old Thunderbird or plow the north forty. Those tools are pretty straightforward, and it's easy to find them. In this chapter, I've tried to include tools that aren't quite as obvious. Some tools are for specific tasks: hacking the Mayan calendar, charting your monthly physical cycles, reviving dead tech, investigating people, exploring virtual environments and stalking the wild orgasm.

Other tools in this chapter are less specific—more internal—meant to grease your synapses and put you in that frictionless thought-mode where new ideas abound. These conceptual-tools include braintuners, special interest groups (SIGs), information on cognitive enhancers, biological supplies, tarot decks, body modification data, extreme fashion accoutrements and more.

There's one more thing to remember when you're checking out this, or any other selection of tools: there's no reason you have to use any tool as the manufacturer intended. Feel free to turn your tools upside down or inside out; run them backwards, rewire them or dissect them and use their guts in other tools. Jimi Hendrix might have permanently changed how we hear the electric guitar, but we would never have had Hendrix if Les Paul hadn't become tired of playing wimpy amplified acoustic guitars. Paul's solution? He slapped a pickup and some metal strings on a railroad tie and *voila*—the world's first solid body electric guitar. The moral of this little tale is simple: "innovation" is just "sabotage" dressed up in a suit and tie.

Modern Primitives

Andrea Juno and V. Vale, editors

1989; 212 pp. $20.99 ppd (CA residents add sales tax) from: RE/Search Publications, 20 Romolo St., Ste. B, San Francisco, CA 94133; 415-362-1465

Through interviews and photos with two dozen people who practice "primitive" body modification such as tattooing and piercing, we learn about the spiritual changes that can come through extreme experiences—such as the pain Fakir Musafar describes when he hung by hooks in his chest in an Indian Sun Dance ritual. Legendary tattooist Ed Hardy talks about his crusade to raise the artistic standards of tattooing, while artist Bill Salmon tells us about having his body marked by 48 different artists. Raelyn Gallina and Sheree Rose talk about body piercing and scarification. From tattoo artist Leo Zulueta (largely responsible for the current interest in tribal tattoos), to rave-meister Genesis P-Orridge, the interviews are fascinating.

Modern Primitives is not a shock rag parading crazies for your amusement. All of the people interviewed are looking for something very simple: a way of fighting back at a mass-production consumer culture that prizes standardization above all else. Through "primitive" modifications, they are taking possession of the only thing any of us will ever really own: our bodies.

Tattootime

#1 & 2 $13 each ; #3 & 4 $18 each; #5 $23 ppd (CA residents add sales tax) from: RE/Search Publications, 20 Romolo St., Ste. B, San Francisco, CA 94133; 415-362-1465

Ed Hardy is arguably the most famous tattooist in the world today. His *Tattootime* is billed as a magazine, but each issue is more like a mini-encyclopedia of the tattoo art. The first issue is particularly good, covering the resurgence of tribal designs. The text is well-written and informative, digging into the philosophy of tattooing, but the most exciting things in *Tattootime* are the dozens of photos of some of the best work by contemporary and historical tattooists.

PFIQ

$40/year (4 issues) from: PFIQ, 2215 R Market St., Ste. 801, San Francisco, CA 94114

body art

Issues #1 - #16 $20 each ppd (CA residents add sales tax) from: RE/Search Publications, 20 Romolo Street, Ste B, San Francisco, CA 94133; 415-362-1465

Tattooing is only one type of body modification. Two magazines, Britain's *body art* and the U.S.'s *PFIQ*, also cover other forms of body manipulations—mostly piercing. The main differences between the piercing and tattoo scenes is that over the last decade tattooing has moved into a more above-ground, almost mainstream context, while the piercing arts, with their close ties to fetishism and the S&M world, remain more overtly sexual.

PFIQ (Piercing Fans International Quarterly) is devoted specifically to piercing, although many of their subjects also sport beautiful tattoos. *body art* takes a more general approach to body modification, looking at tattoos, piercing, fetish clothing and make-up. What makes these magazines compelling is that they prove that imagination is virtually the only limit to how you can redesign and enhance your body.

Fakir Musafar's skin is pierced by dozens of sharpened rods as he bears the "Spears of Shiva" in an Indian Kavandi-bearing ceremony.

Carolina Biological Supply

Catalog $17.95 ppd from: Carolina Biological Supply Co., 2700 York Rd., Burlington, NC 27215; 800-334-5551

Need a fully articulated human skeleton? How about some virus cultures? Or a cat's nervous system mounted under clear plastic?

Carolina Biological Supply is the biggest supplier of biology products in the U.S. If you dissected frogs or examined bones in your school, they probably came from Carolina Biological. The range of bones they have for sale is impressive and includes a variety of mammal, reptile, bird and fish species. You can order many of their

A fully articulated and mounted bush baby skeleton from Carolina Biological Supply.

animal bones in pieces (cheapest), or fully articulated and mounted in display cases (most expensive).

Besides bones, Carolina Biological sells an enormous range of educational books, microscope slides, computer software, posters and lab equipment. You can just collect a few bones, or start your own school.

Maxilla & Mandible, Ltd.

Catalog $10 ppd from: Maxilla & Mandible, Ltd., 451-5 Columbus Ave., New York, NY 10024; 212-724-6173

A gourmet shop for bone collectors. Not only do they have a walk-in shop and mail order business, but they'll repair and clean up your old bones, and build you custom cases. Some of the more exotic bones they carry (when available) come from hippos, giraffes, ostriches and lions. They also carry exotic shells, mounted insects, display cases and T-shirts.

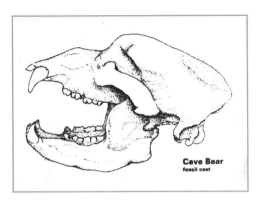

Cave Bear
fossil cast

Bone Room

Catalog free from: Bone Room, 5495 C Claremont Ave., Oakland, CA 94618; 510-652-4286

The Bone Room carries a large variety of mounted insects, animal teeth and skulls, some fully articulated bone sets, and some exotic animal skins (a felt-mounted male lion's skin goes for $5500). They also lease bones by the week. And the Bone Room has a number of plaster fossil casts, everything from a Tyrannosaurus Rex tooth ($14) to a fully articulated giant ground sloth ($33,000).

Skulls Unlimited International

Catalog $4.95 ppd (refundable on first order) from: Skulls Unlimited International, P.O. Box 6741, Moore, OK 73153; 800-659-7585

This outfit specializes in animal skulls. They come in three quality and price levels. First class is for excellent, or "museum quality," specimens, and is the most expensive; second class is "teaching and handling quality," meaning they are in good condition, but may have minor imperfections; third class is "arts and crafts quality," and are mostly for decoration. For some skulls, such as a whitetail buck's, the price can vary widely according to the quality level; a first class whitetail buck skull is $145; second class is $115; third class is $79.

Synergizer

$577 ppd (CA residents add sales tax) from: Inner Technologies, 51 Berry Trail, Fairfax, CA 94930; 800-925-7889

Braintuners and mind machines have been around in various forms for thousands of years. Tibetan monks still use a complex combination of chants (sound) and images (light) in their meditation to break their minds from traditional patterns, and "tune" themselves into a higher consciousness. The Egyptians and some Europeans used the tarot deck this way. More recently, Brion Gysin's *Dream Machine* and Brian Eno's *Oblique Strategies* have served a similar purpose. Now computer tech has entered the realm of altered consciousness.

Your brain wave frequencies are measured in *hertz* (electrical cycles per second). Most tech-based braintuners use some combination of light, sound or electrical impulses to stimulate your brain wave frequencies to get them in tune with the frequencies of the machine. Different hertz levels indicate and control different levels of activity in your brain, from a waking, thinking state to deep, dreamless sleep. At different levels of consciousness, different neurotransmitters and parts of your brain are activated; essentially, you can reach a state associated with traditional meditation.

Why would you want to tune your brain? The answers vary from person to person. Many people claim to have more energy, a better emotional state, enhanced memory, heightened intuition and the ability to control their pain consciously—all benefits associated with yoga and meditation.

The Synergizer is a braintuner with a solid reputation from users. It's a powerful mind machine with 30 built-in programs, but also lets you program your own braintuning sessions. It's also about half the price of comparable machines because it's not a machine unto itself. The Synergizer is a board that plugs into your IBM PC/XT/AT/386 or clone; it comes with an external control box, LED-lined goggles and headphones. It requires DOS 3.3 or above; 512k of RAM and a hard drive are recommended. It comes with all the software, manuals and a 1-year guarantee.

If you want a similar mind machine, but don't have an IBM computer handy, or don't want to deal with switching circuit boards, the MindLab is a comparable high-end machine that goes for $1102 postpaid.

```
┌─────────────────────────────────┐
│                                 │
│                                 │
│   Honour thy error as a hidden intention   │
│                                 │
│                                 │
└─────────────────────────────────┘
```

Oblique Strategies

$35 ppd from: Opal Information, 330 Harrow Rd., London W92 HP, U.K.

The philosopher P.D. Ouspensky once referred to the tarot as a "philosophical machine," meaning that the power of the deck has nothing to do with predicting the future and everything to do with stimulating higher thought processes. Brian Eno and Peter Schmidt's *Oblique Strategies* is a tarot deck for creativity, an oracle waiting to kick you loose from old thinking patterns. Zeroing straight in on your unconscious, the seat of the imagination, the cards offer you advice applicable to any creative act, from washing your car to planning your day to writing a book.

Braintuner Sources

FringeWare, P.O. Box 49921, Austin, TX 78765-9921; 512-477-1366

MegaMind, 10825 Cordova NE, Albuquerque, NM 87112; 800-766-4544

Super Science, P.O. Box 392, Dayton, OH 45409; 513-298-7116

Zentech, P.O. Box 138, Morgan Bay Rd., Surry, ME 04684; 800-659-6031

Organized Obsessions

by Deborah M. Burek & Martin Connors
$9.95; Visible Ink Press
1992; 269 pp.

This is sort of a user-friendly version of the weighty **Encyclopedia of Associations**, and contains contact information for 1,003 organizations, clubs and special interest groups (SIGs). Some of the groups include the Pia Zadora Fan Club, Friends of the Tango, the American Fancy Rat and Mouse Association and the Whirly Girls (an international women's helicopter piloting club).

FAN CLUBS & MORE

AMER (Alliance for Magical and Earth Religions), P.O. Box 16551, Clayton, MO 63105; 314-994-1026

Magical and/or pagan freedom of religion organization.

Betty Scouts of America, Steve Brewster, 2641 S. 53rd St., Kansas City, KS 66106; 913-432-9278; SASE for information

Official Licensed Betty Page fan club; newsletter, T-shirts, cards, etc.

Nick Cave Fan Club, c/o Tender Prey, Ivebury Court, Unit 4, 325 Latimer Road, London, W10 6RA, U.K.; IRC and SAE for info

Musician Nick Cave newsletter and mail order merchandise.

Nina Hartley Fan Club, 1442A Walnut #242, Berkeley CA 94709; $25/year

Adult film star and free speech advocate's fan club; members get autographed photo, filmography, newsletter and merchandise offers.

International Barbie Doll Collectors Club, P.O. Box 79, Bronx, NY 10464; SASE for information

Collects doll data and puts Barbie collectors in touch; newsletter.

James Bond 007 Fan Club, P.O. Box 414, Bronxville, NY 10708; SASE for information.

Kitten Klub; P.O. Box 480513, Los Angeles, CA 90048; $15/year

Charming and sexy star of Russ Meyer films, Kitten Natividad's fan club; members get autographed photo, newsletter and merchandise offers.

Ladies Against Women, 48 Shattuck Sq., #70, Berkeley, CA 94704; SASE for information

Feminist humor group; sponsors "consciousness-lowering" sessions, endangered species fashion show, etc. Newsletter and seminars.

Loyalists of the Vampire Realm, P.O. Box 6975, Beverly Hills, CA 90212-6875; SASE for information

International group to preserve and recreate vampire-style art.

Marx Brothers Study Unit, Darien 28, New Hope, PA 18938; 215-862-9734; SASE for information

Group dedicated to studying and dispensing info on the lives and careers of the Marx Brothers.

Mr. Ed Fan Club, P.O. Box 1009, Cedar Hill, TX 75104; SASE for information

Bestows annual EdWards and runs Museum of Ed; newsletter.

National Association of Fan Clubs, 2730 Baltimore Ave., Pueblo, CO 81003; 303-543-6708; SASE for information

Promotes fan clubs and puts fans in touch with specific clubs.

Nude Office Workers SIG, c/o NOW, P.O. Box 4122, Des Moines, IA 50333-4122; SASE for information

Group that puts nudists in touch with clothing-optional employers.

The Orb, Freepost CV744, 14 Newbold Terrace, Leamington Spa CV32 4BR, England; IRC and SAE for info

The band's newsletter and mail order merchandise arm.

Pink Ladies Social Club, 12439 Magnolia #218, North Hollywood, CA 91607

Run by adult film actresses, this is a watchdog group, and will forward fan mail to many adult film stars.

Robert Tilton Fan Club, Brother Randall, 6102 E. Mockingbird, #374, Dallas, TX 75214; send $1 for info

Club for those obsessed with the high-profile TV preacher.

Sonic Death, P.O. Box 1588, Bloomfield, NJ 07003; 201-420-0238; fax 201-420-6494; SASE for information

Sonic Youth fan club; newsletter and mail order merchandise.

T-Shirt of the Month Club

$30/3 months & 3 T-shirts ($33/XXL T-shirts) from: Freddie Baer, c/o Mystopia, P.O. Box 410151, San Francisco, CA 94141-0151

Each month, illustrator Freddie Baer designs and delivers an original piece of collage art on a T-shirt right to your door. T-shirts come in seven colors (except XXLarge, which only come in white, gray and blue). There's no easier way to make your mailbox and your closet more amusing. The club is limited to 50 members at a time. Write for more information.

Skin Two

$21.45/issue (ppd; CA residents add sales tax) from: Last Gasp, 2180 Bryant, San Francisco, CA 94110; 415-824-6636

The most beautiful, up-to-date and well-written peek into the leather/rubber/vinyl fetish fashion scene. Great photos, plus interviews with designers, and fetish-aware celebs such as The Cramps and author Clive Barker.

Fantasy Fashion Digest

$9.95/issue from: Strictly Speaking Pub., P.O. Box 8006, Palm Springs, CA 92263

This slick zine is the closest thing available to an access guide to the fetish and extreme clothing world. It has ads for companies and stores all over the world with clothes "...that can make you look like the hottest Dominatrix, the sissiest Maid or the most humble submissive...." There are also personal ads in the back.

Mailorder Fashions

Ameba, 1732 Haight St., San Francisco, CA 94117; 800-292-6322; 415-750-9368

Psychedelic and rave-wear shirts, hats and dresses for adults and kids.

B.R. Creations, P.O. Box 4201, Mountain View, CA 94040; 415-961-5354; catalog $5

Custom-made Victorian corsets in materials such as cotton-backed satin, brocade and leather.

Demask, Zeedijk 64, 1012 BA Amsterdam, Holland; catalog $16 (checks in guilders only)

Stylish latex masks and head gear, from the demure to the extreme.

Incognito, 323 S. Main St., P.O. Box 1286, Royal Oak, MI 48067; catalog $2

Dozens of way cool sunglasses, plus Doc Martens shoes and boots.

Intimate Treasures, P.O. Box 77902, San Francisco, CA 94107-0902; 415-896-0944

An adult fashion and entertainment "catalog of catalogs"—from lingerie to leather to fashions for cross-dressers.

Nelson's Kente Cloth Fashions, 536 Welton St., Chula Vista, CA 91911

Real Kente cloth fashions from Ghana—African crowns, vests, shawls, ties, purses, full cloth and more.

Noir Leather U.S.A., 415 S. Main St., Royal Oak, MI 48067; 313-541-3979; video $19.98 ppd

Fashion, jewelry and fetish gear with a punk/gothic bent. *Noir's Sin & Skin Bondage Ball* video is fun and sexy, and features real people who wear the clothes, so it's not all "model" body types. Good products; great attitude.

Pierre Silber Shoes, P.O. Box 265, Saratoga, CA 95071-0265; catalog $2.50

Women's shoes and boots in standard and extra-large sizes for men.

Used Rubber USA, 597 Haight St., San Francisco, CA 94117; 415-626-7855; catalog free

Tire inner tubes get recycled into shoulder bags, appointment books, pouches, saddlebags, etc. Each has a lifetime guarantee.

World Domination, JAF Station, P.O. Box 1099, New York, NY 10116-1099; 212-502-1162

Sexy, high-quality lambskin leather fashions for women.

FringeWare Review

$12/year (4 issues; $16 foreign; $4.50 sample) from: FringeWare Inc., P.O. Box 49921, Austin, TX 78765; 512-477-1366

FringeWare Review is the mutant offspring of some Austin, Texas hackers, and neo-entrepreneurs; it's a combination cyberculture zine and a fringe technology catalog, looking at garage-tech, cyberarts, weird science and products and memes that can only be called "postmodern." Some of the wares they hawk are the now-discontinued Mattel PowerGlove, the GoldBrick interface (which uses the PowerGlove to replace the mouse on your Mac), the IBM-compatible VR demo disk—Virtual Reality Playhouse, extraterrestrial invasion defense kits, CD-ROMs and lots more. One of the nice qualities about *FringeWare Review* is that while they want to move their merchandise, they aren't frantically mercenary about it, and will often mention cool items they don't even carry.

The articles from their first issue include reports from fringe nodes around the world (well, the U.S. and Tokyo), rave coverage, info on cognitive enhancers, DIY tech, book reviews, data encryption, swell toys and lots more.

If you want to know more, and have Internet access, you can subscribe to the FringeWare online mailing list (or jump into online discussions) by emailing a request to:

fringeware-request@wixer.bga.com

Type "subscribe" at the prompt.

PowerGlove

$50 minimum (price rises or falls depending on supply) from: FringeWare Inc., P.O. Box 49921, Austin, TX 78765; 512-477-1366; email: fringeware@wixer.cactus.org

There's no such thing as dead tech anymore. Virtually anything with a chip in it is useful to someone somewhere. Take the Mattel PowerGlove. Originally sold as a video game interface, Mattel soon abandoned it because of high costs and low demand from game players. But the units still existed, the circuitry worked and, as a number of hackers realized, a device that could drive a video game could also drive a computer. A sort of PowerGlove underground has developed through colleges and online systems. People come up with code to let the glove perform tasks, then others build on that. I've seen both computer graphics demos and music performances built around the glove.

For $171 postpaid, FringeWare sells the Gold Brick Nugget, a Macintosh package that turns the glove into a mouse substitute. Another unit, the PGSI (not sold by FringeWare), lets you hook your glove to a Macintosh, IBM or clone, Amiga or any other unit with a RS-232 interface. You can couple the glove with a pair of "SEGA-style" LCD glasses (another game interface) to create a low-end virtual reality system. For more information about the PGSI, email: pgsi@uiuc.edu.

PowerGlove Online Information List

Internet PowerGlove list

email: listserv@boxer.nas.nasa.gov

send message: "get glove README" or "subscribe glove-list your user address"

FringeWare PowerGlove texts

email: fringeware-request@wixer.cactus.org

send message: "get *filename*" to retrieve any of these files:

powglove.faq	PowerGlove for VR - Freq. Asked Questions
brainbox.pub	Jim Brain's PowerGlove interface publicity
pgcable.txt	Nintendo extender cable wiring/availability

The Adult BBS Guidebook

by Billy Wildhack
1993; 126 pp.
$12.50 ppd from: Keyhole Publications, P.O. Box 35, Sycamore, IL 60178

Explore the seamier side of cyberspace with this guidebook to the parts of the global information highway you're not supposed to know about. Over four dozen BBSs are thoroughly profiled, with specs that include which systems have online chat services, downloadable GIF files, personal ads, etc. The book's introduction would be useful to *anyone* new to the BBS world.

Sexual Tools and Toys

by Mary Maxwell

The way I figure it, any task is easier with the proper tools. According to a recent survey, 66% of women between 18 and 30 masturbate on a regular basis. So folks are doing the job—with or without tools. Here are some tools I'd recommend—for playing alone or with a lover.

Silicone Dildos

Don't be shy. Life's too short for that. Let's talk about dildos.

In the Good Vibrations store there are shelves of silicone dildos, standing upright on their flared bases. When a passing customer bumps a shelf, the vibration sets the dildos in motion, and they nod gracefully together. I've never been in the store during an earthquake, but I'd imagine the shelves of dildos work very well as earthquake detectors. They function admirably in other ways as well.

Silicone dildos are practical because they quickly warm up to body temperature, they're flexible and resilient, and they're easy to clean. They come in a variety of shapes and sizes. You can get a dildo that looks like a penis, one that's an abstract, vaguely rounded shaft, or even one that's sculpted as a whale, a dolphin, or a diving woman. And of course, they come in a variety of sizes, from petite to terrifyingly extra jumbo.

That's why they're practical. I'll let you figure out why they're fun. And if your mom finds your dildo in your drawer, you can always explain that it's an earthquake detector.

Hitachi Magic Wand

The Hitachi Magic Wand: Good Vibrations' most popular vibrator. The two-speed Hitachi has a soft, tennis ball-sized head which is equally good for squeezing blissfully between your thighs or for running up and down a sore back. The ideal choice for those who want a vibrator with many uses.

I've had my Hitachi Magic Wand for years and I can testify that it's powerful, reliable, and well-made. Oh, yeah—and it's a lot of fun, too.

The Magic Wand runs on household current. It's a hefty piece of equipment—a head about the size of a tennis ball on a shaft that's about a foot long. Plug it in, and the head will hum merrily along at either of two speeds. For women who want vaginal penetration as well as clitoral massage, I'd recommend buying one of two attachments: either the Wonder Wand or the G-Spotter. These vinyl caps slip over the head of the vibrator. The shaft attached to the vinyl cap (a straight shaft in the case of the Wonder Wand; a gently curved one in the G-Spotter) can provide focused clitoral stimulation or vaginal vibrations. For men who want to try a novel kind of penis stimulation, there's a little shot glass-sized attachment called a "come cup."

Some people find the electrical cord a problem, but you'd be surprised at how quickly you forget it's there. After all, you'll have other things on your mind.

Silicone dildos, from $33.50 to $45.50 ppd; Hitachi Magic Wand, $43.50 ppd (CA residents add sales tax) from: Good Vibrations, 938 Howard St., San Francisco, CA 94103; 415-550-7399; fax 415-550-8495

Good Vibrations Catalog

$2 ($4 for Good Vibrations and Sexuality Library catalogs) from: Good Vibrations, 938 Howard St., San Francisco, CA 94103; 415-550-7399; fax 415-550-8495; retail store: 1210 Valencia St., San Francisco, CA; 12 p.m. to 6 p.m., 7 days

Good Vibrations is the sister operation of the Sexuality Library (see review, page 52). They dispense information, advice and quality sex toys and paraphernalia for men and women of all persuasions. They have everything you might need for adventures of the up close and personal kind—lubricants and bondage essentials, safe sex supplies and edible body paint, vibrators, dildos and harnesses.

Other Sex Tools Catalogs

Eve's Garden, 119 W. 57th St., #420, New York, NY 10019; 212-757-8651; catalog $3

Xandria Collection, P.O. Box 31039, San Francisco, CA 94131; catalog $4

Voyages, c/o Intimate Treasures, P.O. Box 77902, San Francisco, CA 94107-0902; 415-896-0944; catalog $6

Smart Drugs & Nutrients

by Ward Dean, M.D. & John Morgenthaler

1991; 222 pp. $16.95 ppd (CA residents add sales tax; $17.95 Canada; $19.95 overseas) from: B&J Publications, P.O. Box 483-905, Santa Cruz, CA 95061-0483

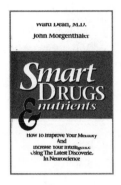

Smart drugs are a class of chemicals that are alleged to give users enhanced cognitive abilities, better memory, etc. Personally, I don't believe that 99% of so-called smart drugs work, and I'm not recommending that you take them. However, if you're going to try them (and I know you are), **Smart Drugs & Nutrients** is a good introductory guide as it comes with little of the propagandizing and rah-rah-we're-the-mutant-edge rhetoric that surrounds the smart drug debate like a halo of gnats. The book discusses new developments in neuroscience, laying out the theoretical basis for smart drugs; it then goes on to explain how to use specific drugs for the best effects. It also has a lengthy list of domestic and overseas mail order addresses that ship substances currently unavailable in the United States. But before you blow a lot of your cash on frontal lobe extenders, remember that the FDA has dropped the hammer on some of the companies listed, and routinely seizes any of their parcels at Customs. Despite that, **Smart Drugs & Nutrients** remains a useful primer for the budding big brain.

• *Physicians are often reluctant to prescribe drugs for cognitive enhancement since it is not an "approved use." In April, 1982, the FDA issued a bulletin which included an important policy statement. The statement clarified the questions about prescribing drugs for "unapproved" uses, stating that physicians may prescribe drugs for unapproved uses in order to provide the best possible health care to the American public. The bulletin clearly stated that the use of "approved" drugs for "unapproved" uses is not only legal, but is one of the primary means of therapeutic innovation.*

Smart Drug Information Sources

Age Reduction Supplements, 8900 Winnetka Ave., #23, Northridge, CA 91324; 800-748-6166; fax 818-407-8500

B. Mougios & Co. O. E., Pittakou 23 T.K., 54645, Tessaloniki, Greece

Discovery Experimental & Development, 29949 S.R. 54 West Wesley, Chapel, FL 33534

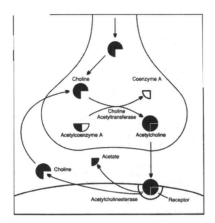

Recycling of choline at the synapse, the site of communication between nerve cells. Many smart drugs, including choline, work by increasing available acetylcholine at the synapse.

Farmacias Roma, P.O. Box 438070, San Diego, CA 92143-8070; fax (Rome) 011-52-66-86-02-35

Fountain Research, P.O. Box 250, Lower Lake, CA 95457; 800-659-1915

Futique Pharmaceuticals, c/o Cybernautech, P.O. Box 121, Monroeville, PA 15146-0121; catalog $9

John Bell & Croyden, 52-54 Wygmore St., London, U.K.; 011-44-71-935-5555

Life Services Supplements, 81 First Ave., Atlantic Highlands, NJ 07716; 800-542-3230

Masters Marketing Co., Ltd., Masters House - No. 1 Marlborough Hill, Harrow Middx. HA1 1TW, England; fax 081-427-1994

Quotaz S.A., P7, 20-21 (Planken), D-6800 Mannheim 1, Germany; catalog free

Qwilleran, P.O. Box 1210, Birmingham, B10 9QA, England

Smart Products, Inc., 870 Market St., #1262, San Francisco, CA 94102; 415-989-2500; fax 415-981-3334; 800-858-6520; catalog free

World Health Services, P.O. Box 20, CH-2822 Courroux, Switzerland

MacJesus

For Macintosh; $10 ppd from: Robert Carr, P.O. Box 2761, Borah Station, Boise, Idaho 83701 (Requirements: Hypercard 1.2.2)

Feel like you need a little spiritual guidance? Maybe a new direction in your life? Feel like you need a guiding hand? Then stay the hell away from MacJesus!

If, however, you're amused by a foul-mouthed, wheezing, evil-tempered allegedly-divine lech with an oral fixation and the ability to lob thunderbolts at will, then this is may be the disk for you, you pervert. Go ahead, ask MacJesus a question. You'll get an answer all right. Ever hear that God works in mysterious ways? Well MacJesus works overtime, and is snide to boot. But if you're even reading this, you're probably half way to hell anyway; you might as well buy the damned (no pun intended) thing and have a few laughs on the way. See you there; I'll be running the paddleboat concession on the lake of fire.

Morph

$95 retail; information free from: Gryphon Software; 7220 Trade St., Ste. 120; San Diego, CA 92121; 619-454-6836; fax 619-454-5329

This is, perhaps the single coolest piece of graphics software to appear in a long time. By now you've probably heard about morphing, or seen it in dozens of commericials; its most famous appearance was in the movie *Terminator 2*. Remember the evil shape-changing cyborg? The computer graphics process used to change him is called morphing.

You used to need about $20,000 worth of hardware to digitally melt one image into another. Now, however, you can perform graphic magic on any Macintosh with enough memory (the program is a memory hog). You can't beat that for about $100 (Requires 5 MB RAM; Macintosh LC II or later; minimum 40 MB hard drive; System 6.0.7 or later, including System 7.0; QuickTime 1.0 [included]).

Mayan Calendrics

For IBM & clones; $58 ppd (TX residents add sales tax) from: Dolphin Software, 4815 W. Braker Ln., Austin, TX 78759; 512-479-9208

This software is indispensable for Maya scholars and for anyone interested in the Maya calendar. It converts dates in the Maya calendar to and from Western dates. Mayan dates may be either dates in the sacred and civil calendars (the so-called tzolkin/haab dates, for example, 13 Imix 19 Kayab) or long count dates (for example, 9.9.16.0.0). Western dates may be expressed in either the Gregorian calendar or the Julian. A date expressed in any calendrical system is automatically converted to dates in all the others (and to the astronomical Julian day number). Arithmetic operations with long count dates are supported.

Mayan Calendrics uses the correlation number (the Julian day number of 0.0.0.0.0 4 Ahau 8 Cumku, which determines the relation between the Maya and Western calendars) recommended by Sir Eric S. Thompson, but allows use of any desired correlation number. The software also allows use of different year-bearer systems (three different year-bearer systems were used by the Mayas at various times and places) and allows specification of the number (0 or 1) of the first day in the Maya haab month. It may thus be used with Maya dates from the Dresden, Paris and Madrid codices and with dates from other sources.

When a tzolkin/haab date is entered, the software displays which year-bearer systems it is consistent with, and allows identification of all Western dates within a given range of years which correspond to that tzolkin/haab date.

Mayan Calendrics Version 3.33 has detailed help and information screens, optional output to printer or disk file and comes with a 37-page explanation and commentary. A 110-item bibliography is included. The software runs on both color and monochrome PCs with DOS 3.00 or later. —Peter Meyer

Menstat

For Macintosh or PC (running Windows); $102 ppd (TX residents add sales tax) from: FringeWare, P.O. Box 49921, Austin TX 78765-9921; 512-477-1366; email: fringeware@wixer.bga.com

Menstat is one of the few computer programs around aimed directly at women. At its simplest, Menstat is a tool for tracking and estimating menstrual cycles; you can, however, use it to track any type of personal cycles. I know women using it to track mood swings, food cravings, zits and their level of sexual arousal.

The basic program resembles a simple spreadsheet, where you enter personal data such as the onset of bleeding, body temperature and changes in mucosity. A Comments section lets you add notes and observations to any part of your cycle.

Bundled with Menstat is a related Hypercard stack called Menstack. This is a reference tool with information about medicinal plants and herbs, exercises, multi-cultural celebrations related to the menstrual cycle, a glossary of medical terms, a bibliography and lists of organizations related to women's concerns.

Beyond Cyberpunk!

For Macintosh; $37.50 ppd from: The Computer Lab, Rt. 4, P.O. Box 54C, Louisa, VA 23093; 703-532-1785; email: gareth@aol.com

This 5.5 megabyte interactive multimedia Hypercard stack uses the guiding metaphor of an information machine, illuminating the world as seen from the edge. Its turf? The interzone where high tech hits the street. This massive stack has essays and hundreds of reviews on postmodern science fiction, critical theory, underground culture, street tech and lots more (over 325 items).

Beyond Cyberpunk! was created by Peter Sugarman and Gareth Branwyn. It features essays and reviews of some of the major figures in science fiction and the emerging cyberculture including Bruce Sterling, Rudy Rucker, Mark Fraunenfelder, Stephen Brown, Hakim Bey, Robert Anton Wilson and Mike Gunderloy. The future's leaking into the present; it's almost here, almost gone. Catch up with the future before it catches up with you! (Requires 2 MB RAM and Hypercard 2.0 or later.) —Paco Xander Nathan

Timewave Zero

For IBM & clones; $64 ppd (TX residents add sales tax) from: Dolphin Software, 4815 W. Braker Ln., Austin, TX 78759; 512-479-9208

Software launching on my DOS system emits its bold meme— "Timewave Zero version 4.07. Copyright 1989, 1991 Lux Natura. A precision instrument for exploring the theory of time as a fractal wave derived from the King Wen Sequence of I Ching Hexagrams. Based on extraterrestrial communications to Terence McKenna. Software developed by Peter Meyer. Published by Dolphin Software. Please press a key to begin..."

Welcome to Time Hacking.

Timewave Zero, as the docs state, "correlates history with the ebb and flow of novelty, which is intrinsic to the structure of the universe." Timewave Zero presents time as a fractal that zig-zags through advances and declines, extropy and habituation, leading to a zero point at 21 Dec 2012. This is a singularity, which corresponds with the end-of-the-line for the Mayan calendar as well. McKenna's work charts Time as the ebb and flow of Novelty and Habit. His friend Rupert Sheldrake cites periods of habituation as morphogenic, i.e. developing form. Their friend Ralph Abraham describes the zero date as a chaotic strange attractor leading to some event or non-event. Maybe 2012 isn't Armageddon, but rather a launching point for an ultra-chaotic suprahistory.

Programmer-au-poil Peter Meyer has done an exquisite job of presenting Timewave Zero on a common denominator PC platform— DOS 2.10 or later without even any graphics adaptor card required. Peter's implementation of Timewave Zero provides a solid, intuitive framework for exploring the time fractal, from any target date or timespan. We sat around an open fire in my backyard one moonful night, sipping a nice cabernet and time traveling....
—Paco Xander Nathan

How To Get Anything On Anybody, Book 2

The Encyclopedia of Personal Surveillance
by Lee Lapin

1991; 232 pp. $36.95 ppd (WA residents add sales tax) from:
Loompanics Unlimited, P.O. Box 1197, Port Townsend, WA 98368

This is the Big Golden Book of Finding Out Things Others Want To Keep Under Wraps. It looks at a wide range of current surveillance and countersurveillance equipment and basic techniques, including audio and video surveillance, secret recording techniques, listening through walls, obtaining restricted phone company information, the proper way to tail a suspect and database cracking. An ABC news reporter called the 1983 version of this guide, "possibly the most dangerous book ever published." Forget the physical assault ethos of **The Anarchist Cookbook** (besides, the recipes are lousy and you'll just blow yourself up); information is the bludgeon of the twenty-first century.

Elsevier Science Publishing

Forensic & Police Science catalog free from: Elsevier Science Publishing, Box 882, Madison Square Station, New York, NY 10159; 212-633-3650

Elsevier Science Publishing is a textbook publisher with an extensive law enforcement imprint. Their books aren't cheap (in the $40 to $60 range), but they are the real thing, used by cops and detective candidates in their training. A few of Elsevier's more intriguing titles are **Practical Homicide Investigation**, **The Counter-Terrorism Handbook**, and **Practical Fire & Arson Investigation**.

Spy Store

Catalog free from: Spy Store, 164 Christopher St., New York, NY 10014; 212-366-6466

Although there are a lot of shops with variations on the name "Spy Store," this is the original, non-chain, surveillance and countersurveillance shop. Their goods are professional quality (that's not just my opinion, but that of surveillance professionals), and the staff knowledgeable. This is one of the few shops in the biz where you will walk out knowing a lot more than you did when you walked in, and you will not get ripped-off in the process.

Counterspy Shop

Video catalog $80 ppd from: Counterspy Shop, 9557 Wilshire Blvd., Beverly Hills, CA 90212; 310-274-6256

These folks not only market, but manufacture the kind of surveillance and counter-surveillance equipment that's absolutely essential for

NIGHTFINDER TH 70
See through dense smoke, fog or total darkness. The TH 70 is a hands-free system that allows you to continue driving, flying or working without light. The light-weight goggles strap around your head to leave the hands free. With its passive light intensification source, the TH 70 needs no more light than a single star.

the Lifestyles of the Rich and Paranoid. If you're in the market for a terrorist-proof limo, tear gas pen, telephone voice scrambler, or night-vision goggles, look no further. Their catalog is a pricey little item, coming in at $80. It's a 40-minute video containing demos of their products, with literature.

U.S. Cavalry

Catalog $3 ($5 foreign) from: U.S. Cavalry, 2855 Centennial Ave., Radcliff, KY 40160-9000; 800-777-7732; fax 502-352-0266

A mail order catalog featuring lots of survival, miltary and law enforcement gear, uniforms and accessories. They have a basic selection of surveillance equipment, such as head-mounted walkie-talkies, listening devices, various binoculars, night-vision scopes and bug detectors. Their law enforcement-type gear includes body armor, hand and wrist restraints, police equipment belts and personal defense devices such as stun guns and tear gas sprays.

AT&T Videophone 2500

Approx. $1000; check phone directory for your local AT&T Phone Center, or call AT&T information: 201-581-3905

We've all wanted one since they first appeared at the 1965 World's Fair. Back then, though, the picture was small, grainy and only black and white. AT&T's consumer videophone has a 3.3-inch active-matrix liquid crystal display, with a clear, crisp image. And it is an analog system, which means that you can plug the 2500 into any existing phone socket, and use it immediately (but remember: you can only see the person on the other end of the line if he or she also has a videophone). When you're speaking to someone who doesn't have a video screen, the 2500 works as a regular phone, and has a built-in microphone, so it doubles as a speakerphone. If you're talking to someone you cannot see, however, you might try the 2500's most unsettling feature: self-viewing. Yes, you can watch yourself watching yourself, all in full color.

To work in real time, the 2500 uses video compression techniques that vary with both the speed and quality of the display. In other words, the closer you want the face on the screen to look like a real face talking to you, the lower the overall quality of the picture will be (this has to do with how fast the video screen can update itself). And during a normal conversation, the display will always be a little out of synch, because the fastest video speed (10 frames per second) isn't quite fast enough to keep up with your face. Still, this is the first consumer-level product that lets you send video over standard phones lines, so it will work with almost any phone system in the world. And with video compression getting better and faster all the time, video communications tools like the 2500 will only get better and cheaper. The $1000 selling price of the 2500, in fact, is a third lower than its original price.

ShareVision

Between $1200-$4500 from: ShareVision Technology, 2951 Zanker Rd., San Jose, CA 95134; 408-428-0330; fax 408-428-9871

Now anyone with a Macintosh computer can have a videophone on their desk. What's more, if the person you're calling is using the same system, you can open and share the same document, making additions and deletions, in real time. Using the "ShareView Plus" system, you can open and share virtually any Mac application over standard phone lines.

The $1200 "ShareView" system gives you audio communications, and lets you share documents and applications; for an additional $3300, you can add video. The system comes with a built-in modem and fax.

The company plans to introduce a Windows version of the ShareView system in late 1993.

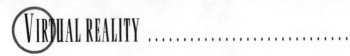

Virtual Reality Online Information

by Bill Cockayne (email: billc@apple.com)

Discussion Groups

Internet

sci.virtual-worlds and sci.virtual-worlds-apps, moderated by Bob Jacobson and Mark A. DeLoura, are the main online VR discussions.

alt.cyberpunk and alt.cyberpunk.tech often concern topics related to VR, though that is not the focus of the discussions themselves.

alt.cyberspace has pretty light-hearted discussions on the present and future implementation of cyberspace in the world.

America Online

The VR discussion on AOL is sponsored by Virtus Corporation and can be found in their directory. To get to the discussion, use the keyword VIRTUS, and look in the "Let's Discuss" folder.

Well

Telnet 192.132.30.2 or use dial up and type 'g vr'

BIX

The BIX conference is moderated by Dan Duncan and can be reached by typing "j virtual.world" There are a number of papers by virtual luminaries such as Bob Jacobson, Brenda Laurel, William Bricken, Brad Smith, Randy Walser and others available on line, as well as some lively discussion about the technical, philosophical, and political impact of VR. BIX can be called on your modem at 800-695-4882 for details and rates.

CompuServe

Once you are on CompuServe, to get to VR type "go graphdev". Look in the VR TECH areas for mail and libraries.

Computer Bulletin Boards

CyberBBS [CA]
510-527-9012 2400 baud

Diaspar Virtual Reality Network [CA]

714-376-1200 2400 baud
714-376-1234 9600 baud

SENSE/NET [UT]

801-364-6227

Toronto Virtual Reality SIG

416-631-6625 16.8K baud

Virtual Space Driver [MD]

301-424-9133

Zarno [GA]

706-860-2927; RIME carrier

DIY VR

by Paco Xander Nathan

Low-end VR boasts a wide array of free software, low-cost hardware and grass-roots development. Dave Stampe and Bernie Roehl of the University of Waterloo distribute REND386, a popular 3D polygon rendering package for DOS (386 and up). Create and fly through animated virtual worlds on a PC, navigating with a joystick or cursor keypad. Import sophisticated world files from high-end VR workstations. Wire up a PowerGlove to replace the joystick, and add a pair of Sega LCD glasses to view worlds in stereo 3D. Complete source code libraries in Turbo C and circuit diagrams are freely available:

sunee.uwaterloo.ca: /pub/rend386 (anonymous FTP site)

rend386-request@sunee.uwaterloo.ca (Internet email list)

Moving up in the world, Jim Brain and Ben Gross of the University of Illinois at Urbana-Champaign have developed the PGSI interface box to connect peripherals like PowerGlove, Sega glasses, etc. into DOS, Mac, Amiga, Windows or just about any computer's serial port, for high-performance 3D. PGSI sells for about $100 in kit form, or slightly more assembled. For information:

ftp.cso.uiuc.edu: /ACM/PGSI (anonymous FTP site)

pgsi@uiuc.edu (email for info)

Mark Pflagling and company at VRASP (the Virtual Reality Alliance of Students and Professionals) use these tools and more to sponsor public demos, workshops and even a CompuServe VR forum. Mark also develops Windows applications which use PowerGlove input, and has been working on low-cost gesture recognition:

VRASP, P.O. Box 4139, Highland Park, NJ 08904; 908-463-8787; 70233.1552@CompuServe.com

Wearable Computers

by Paco Xander Nathan

Laptop/notebook/palmtop spew spearheaded the Incredible Shrinking Computer Revolution with all its digital mobility. However, these metaphors are still Desktops, albeit smaller. Staring at a screen, tapping on a QWERTY, doodling with an input pen— tasks well suited for some measly lab assistant but not for a Mondoid on the run, desperately busy at work/trouble/play.

Enter homebrew hack Douglas Platt of Select Tech, "Eventually, I don't see any reason for having a desktop." Platt backs his words with awesome specs: 386 25MHz, up to 8 Mb RAM, standard PC ports, rugged 120 Mb drive, Private Eye display (3 oz. heads-up display, appears as full 720 x 280 screen floating transparently in space), with a battery life of 4 hours. "My present unit is mounted in a fanny pack—weighs about four pounds with batteries." Costs about $3500. The BFD is you get to wear Platt's system, which leaves limbs free to fulfill a human side of the emerging cyborg equation.

Use a computer without having to lock your butt in a chair or fuse both hands to a QWERTY keyboard nightmare. A small seven-key, one-handed chord keyboard allows rapid touch-typing, with a one hour learning curve for basic letters, numbers and punctuation. Tack on a cellular or wireless modem, and *voila!* Squidheads can now jack into the Net and still be free to carry luggage, open a door, execute fire and maneuver ops, etc. Platt is also developing headset cellular/wireless phones to add in hands-free voice: "You can literally be standing in the rain, holding an umbrella, handling a customer service call."

Rumor has it that certain Japanese firms, such as NEC, are heading down similar lines. "We are thinking about personal environment design—architecture for the human environment," says Hideji Takemasa of NEC's Advanced PC Design Center in Tokyo. Specs for several NEC wearables in development have been released, including portable offices, emergency medic assists, satellite links, etc. Takemasa-san notes an important design point: "There are no preconceptions as to how they'll look or work." NEC plans to introduce a "Hands-Off" phone module in '93 (to be worn on the wrist) then advance into more sophisticated wearable designs.

Expect Select Tech to offer kits with software, or full wearable units

(top) NEC's proposed Porto Office lets users input data with a keyboard, LCD writing pad or microphone; the system comes with a built-in fax, 35 mm camera and speakerphone.

(left) The TLC Computer lets medics take a patient's signs, visually scan the patient with a built-in videocam, describe the patient's condition into a microphone, and transmit the data to the hospital. An eyeglass heads-up display shows the same information to the medic.

in 1993. "The purpose of the shareware, TryChorder 1.1, is to popularize chording on the desktop, to teach potential *HIP PC* users how to chord...." Target applications for his wearable will be content-based: encyclopedias, public domain books, biofeedback, suggestion software, idea developers: "Software to augment your intelligence, change your states, etc." So that we can transit lifestyles into the cyborgs we lust to become.

Select Tech, Inc.

Douglas Platt, 1657 The Fairway, #151, Jenkintown, PA 19046; 215-277-4264; email: dplatt@cellar.org

NEC U.S. Communications Office

Kazuko Andersen, 280 Park Ave, 21 East, New York, NY 10017; 212-972-2046; fax 212-972-2044

Bellcore Catalog of
Technical Information

Catalog free from: Information Exchange Management, Bellcore, 445 South St., Rm 2J-125, P.O. Box 1910, Morristown, NJ 07962-1910; 800-521-2673; fax 908-699-0936; foreign calls 908-699-5800

For all you eager young phone phreaks, this is the motherlode. Straight from the Bell communications center, comes the Bellcore catalog. Broken down by regional phone providers (Ameritech, Bell Atlantic, Bellsouth, Nynex, Pacific Bell, and Bellcore itself), you can get all the technical data you need—well, to understand how your phone company works, from switching systems to wooden telephone pole specs.

Papa Jim Botanica

Catalog free from: Papa Jim Botanica, P.O. Box 14128, San Antonio, TX 78214; 210-922-6665

A mail order source of incense, perfumes and magic talismans, jewelry and books. They also carry what appears to be every tarot deck ever created—a full 25 catalog pages worth. Unfortunately, they don't take checks, but they do take charge cards and will ship COD.

Pacific Coast Sports

Information free from: Superstars Pro Wrestling Training Camp, c/o Pacific Coast Sports, 21063 Cabot Blvd., #1, Hayward, CA 94545; 510-785-8396; fax 510-785-5758

Sure you laugh at Hulk Hogan, Randy "The Macho Man" Savage and other big time pro wrestlers, but in your heart of hearts, didn't you wonder just what it was like to be 300 pounds, dressed in sequined tights, and wrapping your opponent up in a perfectly executed figure-four leglock? Now you can get up close and personal with the mat, and maybe your true destiny. For around $5500 (half the price of many other wrestling schools), Pacific Coast Sports will train you in the basic skills and moves to be a professional wrestler. What's more, if you have any real ability, they'll act as your agents, getting you real bouts with other up-and-coming young mat demons like yourself. If you're interested, you should be in good health, and between 18 and 32 years old.

Aiwa HV-M110

Approx. $550; for your nearest Aiwa dealer call: 800-289-2492

This is a great VCR for business, education or any individual who have ever received or traded a videocassette with someone from

overseas. Videocassette recording and playback standards are different throughout the world. PAL is the system most widely used in Europe, although eastern Europe still uses MESECAM. The U.S. standard is NTSC, but there are two of those! The Aiwa HV-M110 is a truly a multilingual machine; it can convert PAL to NTSC, or vice versa; it can also playback and record cassettes in MESECAM, NTSC 3.58 or NTSC 4.43.

The big brother of the HV-M110 is the HV-M360; for about $100 more, you can get the conversion power of the M110, but with a built-in television tuner, so that you can leave the M360 hooked to your TV for day-to-day recording.

Custom Viewer

Information free from: Custom Viewer, P.O. Box 655, Topanga, CA 90290; 800-669-8439

TV Guide is fine for basic TV watching, but what if you want to know what movie they'll be trashing on "Mystery Science Theater 3000," or when the next "Columbo" re-run is going to play? If you live in a large city with cable TV, you probably receive channels that aren't even listed in any guides. Custom Viewer fixes that. You tell them what you want to know about and they'll email or fax the information straight to you. They can also perform online searches of old shows by title, director, actors, keywords, etc.

INDEX

INDEX

INDEX

· ·